POEMS.

BY

WILL. M. CARLETON.

CHICAGO:
LAKESIDE PUBLISHING AND PRINTING COMPANY.
1871.

THIS LITTLE VOLUME

IS

REVERENTLY AND AFFECTIONATELY

Dedicated

TO

MY FATHER AND MOTHER.

RIFTS IN THE CLOUD.

Life is a cloud!—e'en take it as you may;
Illumine it with Pleasure's transient ray;
Brighten its edge with Virtue; let each fold
E'en by the touch of God be flecked with gold,
While angel-wings may kindly hover near,
And angel-voices murmur words of cheer,
Still, life's a cloud! forever hanging nigh,
Forever o'er our winding pathways spread,
Ready to blacken on some saddened eye,
And hurl its bolts on some defenceless head!

Yes, there are lives that seem to know no ill;
Paths that seem straight, with naught of thorn or
hill;
The bright and glorious sun, each welcome day,
Flashes upon the flowers that deck their way,
And the soft zephyr sings a lullaby,
'Mid rustling trees, to please the ear and eye;
And all the darling child of fortune needs,
And all he cares, and all he knows or heeds,

While fairy eyes their watch above him keep,
Is breath to live, and weariness to sleep.
But life's a cloud! and soon the smiling sky
May wear the unwelcome semblance of a frown,
And the fierce tempest, madly rushing by,
May raise its dripping wings, and strike him down!

When helpless infancy, for love or rest,
Lies nestling to a mother's yearning breast,
While she, enamored of its ways and wiles
As mothers only are, looks down and smiles,
And spies a thousand unsuspected charms
In the sweet babe she presses in her arms,
While he, the love-light kindled in his eyes,
Sends to her own, electrical replies,
A ray of sunshine comes for each caress,
From out the clear blue sky of happiness.
But life's a cloud! and soon the smiling face
The frowns and tears of childish grief may know,
And the love-language of the heart give place
To the wild clamor of a baby's woe.

The days of youth are joyful in their way;
Bare feet tread lightly, and their steps are gay.
Parental kindness grades the early path,
And shields it from the storm-king's dreaded wrath.
But there are thorns that prick the infant flesh,
And bid the youthful eyes to flow afresh,

Thorns that maturer nerves would never feel,
With wounds that bleed not less, that soon they
heal.
When we look back upon our childhood days,
Look down the long and sweetly verdant ways
Wherein we gaily passed the shining hours,
We see the beauty of its blooming flowers,
We breathe its fresh and fragrant air once more,
And, counting all its many pleasures o'er,
And giving them their natural place of chief,
Forget our disappointments, and our grief.
Sorrows that now were light, then weighed us
down,
And claimed our tears for every surly frown.
For life's a cloud, e'en take it as we will,
The changing wind ne'er banishes or lifts!
The pangs of grief but make it darker still,
And happiness is nothing but its rifts!

There is a joy in sturdy manhood, still;
Bravery is joy; and he who says I WILL,
And turns, with swelling heart, and dares the
fates,
While firm resolve upon his purpose waits,
Is happier for the deed; and he whose share
Is honest toil, pits that against dull care.
And yet, in spite of labor, faith, or prayer,
Dark clouds and fearful o'er our paths are driven;
They take the shape of monsters in the air,
And almost shut our eager gaze from Heaven!

Disease is there, with slimy, loathsome touch,
With hollow, blood-shot eyes and eager clutch,
Longing to strike us down with pangs of pain,
And bind us there, with weakness' galling chain.
Ruin is there, with cunning ambush laid,
Waiting some panic in the ranks of trade,
Some profitless endeavor, or some trust
By recreant knave abused, to snatch the crust
From out the mouths of them we love the best,
And bring gaunt hunger, an unwelcome guest.
Disgrace is there, of honest look bereft,
Truth in his right hand, slander in his left,
Pride in his mouth, the devil in his eye,
His garment truth, his cold black heart a lie,
Forging the bolts to blast some honored name;
Longing to see some victim wronged or wrong;
To see him step into the pool of shame,
Or plashed by loved ones that to him belong.

A dark cloud hovers over every zone,
The cloud of ignorance. The great unknown,
Defying comprehension, still hangs low
Above our feeble minds. When we* who now
Have stumbled 'neath the ever-varying load
That marks the weary student's royal road,
Have hurried over verbs in headlong haste,
And various thorny paths of language traced,
Have run our muddled heads, with rueful sigh,

*Class of '69, Hillsdale College, of which this Poem was one of the Graduating Exercises.

'Gainst figures truthful, that yet seemed to lie;
Have peeped into the Sciences, and learned
How much we do not know—have bravely turned
Our guns of eloquence on forest trees,
And preached grave doctrines to the wayward
breeze—
When we have done all this, the foggy cloud,
With scarce a rift, is still above us bowed;
And we are children, on some garden's verge,
Groping for flowers the opposing wall beneath,
Who, flushed and breathless, may at last emerge,
With a few scanty blossoms for a wreath.

But never was a cloud so thick and black,
But it might some time break, and on its track
The glorious sun come streaming. Never, too,
So but its threads might bleach to lighter hue,
Was sorrow's mantle of so deep a dye.
And he who, peering at the troubled sky,
Looks past the clouds, or looks the cloud-rifts
through,
Or, finding none, remembers their great worth,
And strikes them for himself, is that man who
Shows the completest wisdom of this earth.

When one stands forth in Reason's glorious light,
Stands in his own proud consciousness of right,
Laments his faults, his virtues does not boast,
Studies all creatures—and himself the most,
Knowing the way wherewith his faults to meet,

*

Or, vanquished by them, owning his defeat,
He pays the penalty as should a man,
And pitches battle with the foe again;
When, giving all their pro per due and heed,
He yet has power, when such shall be the need,
To go his way, unshackled, true, and free,
And bid the world go hanged, if needs must be,
He strikes a rift for his unfearing eye,
Through the black cloud of low servility:
A cloud that's decked the Orient all these years;
'Neath whose low-bending folds, 'mid groans and
tears,
Priestcraft has heaped its huge, ill-gotten gains,
And tyrants forged their bloody, clanking chains;
A cloud, that when the Mayflower's precious cup
The misty, treacherous deep held proudly up,
By waves that leaped and dashed each other o'er,
But onward still the ark of Freedom bore,
Some fair and peaceful Ararat to find,
Dipped its black wings, and swept not far behind.
To-day, it lowers o'er this great, free land,—
O'er farms and work-shops, offices and spires—
Its baleful shadow casts on every hand,
And darkens church, and state, and household
fires.

It is a thing to pity and to blame,
A useless, vile, humiliating shame,
A silent slander on the Heaven-born soul,
Decked with the signet of its own control,

A flaw upon the image of our God,
When men, obedient to some Mogul's nod—
When men, the sockets of whose addled brains
Are blessed with some illuminate remains
Wherefrom the glim of reason still is shed,
Blow out the light, and send their wits to bed;
And, taking as their sole dictator, then,
Some little, thundering god of speech or pen,
Aping submissively the smile or frown
Of some great brazen face that beats them down,
Or silenced by some lubricated tongue,
Covered with borrowed words and neatly hung—
They yield their judgments up to others' wills,
And take grave creeds like sugar-coated pills;
And, with their weakness tacitly confessed,
Like the unfeathered fledglings of a nest,
When the old bird comes home with worms and flies—
With half a smile and half a knowing frown,
They open wide their mouths, and shut their eyes,
And seem to murmur softly, "*Drop it down.*"

He who will creep about some great man's feet,
The honeyed fragrance of his breath to meet,
Or follow him about, with crafty plan,
And cringe for smiles and favors, is no man.
A fraction of a man, and all his own,
Although his numerator be but one,
With unity divided up so fine
That thousands range themselves beneath the line,

Yet ominously silent; moving on,
While from its threatening folds, so deep and dark,
The forkéd lightning, ever and anon,
Shoots for some life, and never fails its mark!

STEWARD, our classmate, is not here to-day;
Many an oak is blasted on its way,
Many a growing hope is overthrown.
What *might* have been, his early growth had shown;
What *was*, our love and tears for him may tell;
He lived, he toiled, he faded, and he fell.
When STEWARD lay within that narrow room
Men call a coffin—in its cheerless gloom
Himself the only tenant, and asleep
In a long slumber, terrible and deep;
When at the open door his pale, sad face
Appeared to us, without a look or trace
Of recognition in its ghastly hue,
Soon to be hid forever from our view;
When, with his sightless eyes to Heaven up-turned,
Wherefrom his royal soul upon them burned,
He waited for his last rites to be said,
With the pathetic patience of the dead;
When tenderly his manly form we lay
In its last couch, with covering of clay;
Who in that mournful duty had a part,
But felt the cloud of Death upon his heart?

Yet ominously silent; moving on,
While from its threatening folds, so deep and dark,
The forkéd lightning, ever and anon,
Shoots for some life, and never fails its mark!

STEWARD, our classmate, is not here to-day;
Many an oak is blasted on its way,
Many a growing hope is overthrown.
What *might* have been, his early growth had shown;
What *was*, our love and tears for him may tell;
He lived, he toiled, he faded, and he fell.
When STEWARD lay within that narrow room
Men call a coffin—in its cheerless gloom
Himself the only tenant, and asleep
In a long slumber, terrible and deep;
When at the open door his pale, sad face
Appeared to us, without a look or trace
Of recognition in its ghastly hue,
Soon to be hid forever from our view;
When, with his sightless eyes to Heaven upturned,
Wherefrom his royal soul upon them burned,
He waited for his last rites to be said,
With the pathetic patience of the dead;
When tenderly his manly form we lay
In its last couch, with covering of clay;
Who in that mournful duty had a part,
But felt the cloud of Death upon his heart?

But when we thought how his unfettered soul,
Free from his poor sick body's weak control,
Pluming its wings at the Eternal throne,
Might take through realms of space its rapid flight,
And find a million joys to us unknown,
The cloud was rifted by a ray of light.

Old Class of '69! together, still,
We've journeyed up the rough and toilsome hill;
Seeking the gems to labor ne'er denied,
Plucking the fruits that deck the mountain-side.
Now, in the glory of this Summer's day,
We part, and each one goes his different way.
Let each, with hope to fire his yearning soul,
Still hurry onward to the shining goal.
The way at times may dark and weary seem,
No ray of sunshine on our path may beam,
The dark clouds hover o'er us like a pall,
And gloom and sadness seem to compass all;
But still, with honest purpose, toil we on;
And if our steps be upright, straight and true,
Far in the East a golden light shall dawn,
And the bright smile of God come bursting through.

DEATH-DOOMED.

They're taking me to the gallows, mother—they mean
to hang me high;
They're going to gather round me there, and watch
me till I die;
All earthly joy has vanished, now, and gone each
mortal hope,—
They'll draw a cap across my eyes, and round my
neck a rope;
The crazy mob will shout and groan—the priest will
read a prayer.
The drop will fall beneath my feet and leave me in
the air.
They think I murdered Allen Bayne; for so the Judge
has said,
And they'll hang me to the gallows, mother—hang
me till I'm dead!

The grass that grows in yonder meadow, the lambs
that skip and play,

The pebbled brook behind the orchard, that laughs
upon its way,
The flowers that bloom in the dear old garden, the
birds that sing and fly,
Are clear and pure of human blood, and, mother, so
am I!
By father's grave on yonder hill—his name without a
stain—
I ne'er had malice in my heart, or murdered Allen
Bayne!
But twelve good men have found me guilty, for so the
Judge has said,
And they'll hang me to the gallows, mother—hang
me till I'm dead!

The air is fresh and bracing, mother; the sun shines
bright and high;
It is a pleasant day to live—a gloomy one to die!
It is a bright and glorious day the joys of earth to
grasp—
It is a sad and wretched one to strangle, choke, and
gasp!
But let them damp my lofty spirit, or cow me if they
can!
They send me like a rogue to death—I'll meet it like
a man.
For I never murdered Allen Bayne! but so the Judge
has said,
And they'll hang me to the gallows, mother—hang
me till I'm dead!

Poor little sister 'Bell will weep, and kiss me as I lie;
But kiss her twice and thrice for me, and tell her not
to cry;
Tell her to weave a bright, gay garland, and crown me
as of yore,
Then plant a lily upon my grave, and think of me no
more.
And tell that maiden whose love I sought, that I was
faithful yet;
But I must lie in a felon's grave, and she had best
forget.
My memory is stained forever; for so the Judge has
said,
And they'll hang me to the gallows, mother—hang
me till I'm dead!

Lay me not down by my father's side; for once, I
mind, he said
No child that stained his spotless name should share
his mortal bed.
Old friends would look beyond his grave, to my dis-
honored one,
And hide the virtues of the sire behind the recreant
son.
And I can fancy, if there my corse its fettered limbs
should lay,
His frowning skull and crumbling bones would shrink
from me away;
But I swear to God I'm innocent, and never blood
have shed!

And they'll hang me to the gallows, mother—hang
me till I'm dead!

Lay me in my coffin, mother, as you've sometimes
seen me rest:
One of my arms beneath my head, the other on my
breast.
Place my Bible upon my heart—nay, mother, do not
weep—
And kiss me as in happier days you kissed me when
asleep.
And for the rest—for form or rite—but little do I reck;
But cover up that cursèd stain—*the black mark on
my neck!*
And pray to God for his great mercy on my devoted
head;
For they'll hang me to the gallows, mother—hang
me till I'm dead!

* * * * * * *

But hark! I hear a mighty murmur among the jostling
crowd!
A cry!—a shout!—a roar of voices!—it echoes long
and loud!
There dashes a horseman with foaming steed and
tightly-gathered rein!
He sits erect!—he waves his hand!—good Heaven!
'tis Allen Bayne!
The lost is found, the dead alive, my safety is achieved!

For he waves his hand again, and shouts, "The prisoner is reprieved!"
Now, mother, praise the God you love, and raise your drooping head;
For the murderous gallows, black and grim, is cheated of its dead!

UP THE LINE.

Through blinding storm and clouds of night,
We swiftly pushed our restless flight;
With thundering hoof and warning neigh,
We urged our steed upon his way
Up the line.

Afar the lofty head-light gleamed;
Afar the whistle shrieked and screamed;
And glistening bright, and rising high,
Our flakes of fire bestrewed the sky,
Up the line.

Adown the long, complaining track,
Our wheels a message hurried back;
And quivering through the rails ahead,
Went news of our resistless tread,
Up the line.

The trees gave back our din and shout,
And flung their shadow-arms about;
And shivering in their coats of gray,
They heard us roaring far away
          Up the line.

The wailing storm came on apace,
And dashed its tears into our face;
But steadily still we pierced it through,
And cut the sweeping wind in two,
          Up the line.

A rattling rush across the ridge,
A thunder-peal beneath the bridge;
And valley and hill and sober plain
Re-echoed our triumphant strain,
          Up the line.

And when the Eastern streaks of gray
Bespoke the dawn of coming day,
We halted our steed, his journey o'er,
And urged his giant form no more,
          Up the line.

TO JOE, AT WAR.

(1865.)

Now many a day has passed away
  Since last I pressed your hand,
And saw you go to fight the foe
  Of this, our native land.
Thrice has December's chilling blast
Its desolation round you cast,
  Bidding all warmth depart;
And yet I know, my gallant Joe,
  It has not cooled your heart!

Now many a sun has come and gone,
  Since you and I have met,
And deep in gore to rise no more
  Full many a star has set;
A thousand hopes that then were bright
Have darkened into endless night,
  A thousand hearts have bled;
And many a home is wrapped in gloom,
  And mourning for its dead.

Now many a form, once blithe and warm,
  Lies 'neath the Southern sod,
And many a soul has reached the goal,
  And gone to meet its God.
The rolling drum and bugle's tones,
Are freighted with the widow's groans,
  And orphan's helpless cry;
For in the graves of Freedom's braves
  The hearts of thousands lie.

But by the blood of those who stood
  And fought at Bunker Hill,
By all our pride of those who died,
  But live, in history, still;
By all our fields, with carnage stained,
By all that we have lost and gained,
  By all our faith in God,
That flag shall yet be firmly set
  On every Southern rod!

That flag shall float, though o'er the throat
  Of many a blazing gun!
That flag shall wave, though o'er the grave
  Of many a traitorous son!
Though the whole South, from shore to shore,
Be drenched with patriotic gore,
  The North with widows' tears;
Noble and grand that flag shall stand,
  And wave a thousand years!

Full well you know, my honest Joe,
  How virtue e'er exalts;
So may you claim a soldier's fame,
  But shun a soldier's faults.
And when this bloody war is o'er,
And Peace comes smiling down once more
  To heal our nation's woe,
May Honor crown you with renown,
  As gayly home you go.

THE CABLE.

Peal the clanging bell!
  Thunder the brazen gun!
Over the earth in triumph swell
  The notes of a victory won!
Not over field and ditch and corse;
Not by musketry, cannon and horse;
Not by skirmishes bloody and fell;
Not by the whiz of shot and shell;
But men of will and thought,
  Men of muscle and brain,
Have planned and toiled and suffered and
    fought,
  And conquered the raging main!

Far from an Eastern shore,
  By the second ark is brought,
Spanning the dusky distance o'er,
  A line of glowing thought!
Dashing through ripples and torrents and waves,
Courting the gloom of mariners' graves;
Hastily threading the ocean aisles,
And bringing to naught three thousand miles!
For men of will and thought,
  Men of muscle and brain,
Have planned and toiled and suffered and
    fought,
  And conquered the raging main!

Time in his car, indeed,
  Flits fast from place to place;
But restless Thought has dared his speed,
  And Thought has won the race!
Man is as naught in Time's fierce clasp,
But Thought can escape his greedy grasp;
And Time shall have perished, by and by,
But the soul of Thought can never die!
  Thunder the guns as you ought!
    Well may the church bells chime!
  For man, with the Heaven-given sword of thought,
    Has conquered the Scythe of Time!

  Sing to the GOD of love!
    A thousand anthems raise!
  Render to Him who reigns above,
    A tribute of song and praise!
His is the ocean, deep and dark;
His is the quick electric spark;
His is each willing, helping hand;
His are the mighty souls that planned!
  Pray that the blessed line
    May stretch from shore to shore,
  And together the hearts of nations twine,
    Till nations are no more!

JOHN CHINAMAN IS COMING.

From out the sunset's golden flame
  He long has wrapped around him,
From out the walls of woe and shame
  Where centuries have bound him,
With clashing cymbals, opium pipes,
  And horrid words and letters,
With streaming cue, and bleeding stripes,
  And marks of chains and fetters,
With shaven poll, and browless eye,
  And ceaseless sound of drumming,
With rattish rush and hungry cry,
  John Chinaman is coming!

Now drape with crape our spangled flag,
  And vent your righteous passions,
And let your tongues in anger wag,
  American Caucasians!
'Twas sad to roil the Saxon stream
  With Sambo, poor old fellow;

And now, forsooth, its struggling gleam
  Must bear a tinge of yellow!
Yet ere, as freemen, we revile,
  Our conscience craves benumbing;
And 'mid our musings, all the while
  John Chinaman is coming!

Now ye who toil, with quickened breath
  And hotly streaming faces,
And hate the wretch who flees from death
  And cheaply seeks your places,
See, riding down your iron streets,
  In search of warmth and victual,
A man who works for what he eats,
  And only eats a little!
But Western acres long shall grow,
  And factories swell their humming,
And all shall live and prosper, though
  John Chinaman is coming!

Now ye who crush the cringing man,
  And cheat and spurn and spite him,
See here a beast of trampled clan,
  That licks the hands that smite him!
But hold the pearls of your abuse,
  And let your wits befriend you,
Or he you put to shameful use,
  May some time turn and rend you;
For burdened wights to upright forms
  The hand of Right is plumbing,

And straight and proud, through sneers and
storms,
John Chinaman is coming!

Now ye who constant effort wield
To Christianize your neighbors,
Here opens up to you a field
Well worthy of your labors!
And not without allowance due
These threads of vice unravel,
Nor heathen spurn who come to you,
And save you leagues of travel;
And when at last at Heaven's gate
Your passports you are thumbing,
Perhaps you'll see that while you wait,
John Chinaman is coming!

And while our race, that God has made
To work His grandest pleasure,
Climbs slowly to its destined grade,
With steady step and measure;
If, after all our woe and sin,
And weakness and dejection,
The gracious Lord shall let us in
Through gates of blest perfection,
While marching on, and truths Divine
Continually summing,
We'll see that somewhere in the line,
John Chinaman is coming!

THE LABORING MEN.

Who are the laboring men?
We are the laboring men;
We, the muscle of tribes and lands,
With streaming faces and hardened hands;
With well-patched garments, stained and coarse,
With untrained voices, heavy and hoarse;
We, who can brave the noontide heats,
And mow the meadows and pave the streets;
Who hew the timber and turn the sod;
Who wield the hoe and carry the hod;
Yes, we are the laboring men—
The genuine laboring men!
And each, somewhere in the stormy sky,
Has a glittering star, be it low or high!
For pride have we, to do and dare,
And love have we, to cherish and care;
And power have we; for lose our brawn,
And where were your flourishing cities gone?
Or bind our hands or fetter our feet,
And what would the great world find to eat?
Ay, where were your gentry then?
We are the laboring men!

Who are the laboring men?
We are the laboring men!
We who stand in the ranks of trade,
And count the tallies that toil has made;
Who guard the coffers of wealth untold,
And ford the currents of glistening gold;
Who send the train in its hurrying trips,
And rear the stores and own the ships;
And though our coats be a trifle fine,
And though our diamonds flash and shine,
Yet we are the laboring men—
The genuine laboring men!
We guard the gates of the angry seas;
We hold the nation's granary keys;
The routes of trade we have marked and planned,
Are veins of life to a hungry land.
And power have we in our peaceful strife;
For the nation's trade is the nation's life;
And take the sails of our commerce in,
Where were your "laborers' pails of tin"?
Ay, where were your "laborers" then!
We are the laboring men!

Who are the laboring men?
We are the laboring men;
We of the iron and watery way,
Whom fire and steam and tide obey;
Who pierce the sea with a prow of oak,
Who blot the sky with a cloud of smoke;
Who bend the breezes unto our wills,

And work the looms and hurry the mills;
Who oft have the lives of a thousand known,
In the hissing valves that hold our own;
　　Yes, we are the laboring men—
　　The genuine laboring men!
And though a coat may a button lack,
And though a face be sooty and black,
And though an oath in a speech may blend,
A heart's a heart, and a friend's a friend!
And power have we; but for our skill,
The wave would drown, and the sea would kill;
　　And where were your gentry then?
　　Aye, we are the laboring men!

　　Who are the laboring men?
　　We are the laboring men;
We of the mental toil and strain,
Who stall the body and lash the brain;
Who wield the pen when the world's asleep,
And plead with mortals to laugh or weep;
Who bind the wound and plead the cause,
And preach the sermons and make the laws;
Who stand before the listening throng,
And fight the devils of Shame and Wrong;
　　Yes, we are the laboring men—
　　The genuine laboring men!
And though our hands be small and white,
And though our flesh be tender and light,
And though our muscle be soft and low,
Our boiling blood has a mighty flow!

We've power to kindle Passion's fire,
With the flame of rage, and fell desire;
Or quell, with soothing words and arts,
To throbs of grief, the leaping hearts.
        Who shall question, then,
        That we are the laboring men?

        Who are NOT the laboring men?
        They're not the laboring men;
They who creep in dens and lanes,
To rob their betters of honest gains;
The rich that stoop to wrong the poor;
The tramps that beg from door to door;
The rogues who love a darkened sky,
And steal and rob and cheat and lie;
The loafing wights and senseless bloats,
Who drain their pockets to wet their throats!
        They're not the laboring men,
        The genuine laboring men!
And each, some time in the coming days,
Shall stand in the world's indignant gaze;
And each at the bar of the Judge shall stand,
And render account to the Sovereign Land;
And each should be sent to the prison grim,
To toil for the men who have suffered by him;
And there, with a home behind the grate,
Be made to avenge the injured State.
        Truly and justly, then,
        They will be laboring men!

*

A TRIBUTE TO DICKENS.

Across the foaming sea of words and thought,
  Where heavier craft were struggling with the storm,
The winds one day an unknown vessel brought,
  Of flaunting streamer and fantastic form.
Old captains gazed, and wondered at her route,
And gravely shook their grizzled heads in doubt;
And critics nursed their literary ire,
And quickly loaded up their guns to fire.

But crowding sail, she cut the dangerous waves,
  Swept past old wrecks and signals of distress,
And o'er forgotten hulks and nameless graves,
  Straight glided to the harbor of success!
The great World gazed on her a little while,
Its careworn face grew brighter with a smile,
Until its voice caught rapture from its gaze,
And swelled into a thunder-peal of praise!

The outstript jester, smiling, dropped his pun,
  The sage looked up, with laughter in his eyes;
The critic turned his double-shotted gun,
  And jubilantly fired it at the skies!
The laboring throng, when their day's toil was o'er,
Crowded along the unaccustomed shore,
And viewed, with wonder and delight oft-told,
The varied treasures of her deck and hold!

For there, upon the deck, in genial state,
  Stood Pickwick, captain of the motley crew;
The sturdy Samuel Weller for his mate,
  And many a passenger The People knew;
And stored among her cargo of rich mirth,
Shone forth the richest diamonds of earth;
Wit, humor, pathos—all the brighter gems,
Set in a thousand flashing diadems!

And ever as they gazed, and rushed to gaze,
  Came sweeping o'er the sea another gale,
And gleamed upon their glad eyes, thro' the haze,
  The snowy whiteness of another sail;
Rich loaded was one bark, and fair to see,
But aimed great guns at petty tyranny;
And as she swiftly glided safe to land,
Young Captain Nickleby was in command.

Then came a ship of stranger seeming still,
  With "Curiosities" in plenty stored;

And thousands crowded round her, with one will,
  To view the passengers she had on board.
And one there was—her name was "Little Nell"—
The People much admired, and loved full well;
And many wept, and lingered at her side,
When peacefully she laid her down and died.

So one by one to port the vessels came,
  Laden with comfort for both rich and poor,
But hurling bolts of scorn-envenomed flame
  At tyrant, rogue, and snob, and titled boor.
And each new ship the multitude flocked round,
And gloated o'er the treasures that they found;
And as each sail came flashing into sight,
Broke forth a thousand plaudits of delight!

Pictures there were, that painter's brush might pine
  And pray to spring from out its striving art;
The hand that drew their outlines was divine—
  It was the servant of a god-like heart.
The city haunts, from palace down to den,
Stood forth in glowing colors once again;
And the wide country landscape well was traced,
With river, grove, and hill, and desert waste.

And words—such fitly-spoken words as well
  Were to such pictures apples of fine gold,
Upon the ears of listening millions fell,
  And often by the fireside were retold.
Pity, and love, and sympathy, were there;

Sorrow, and rage, and raven-winged despair;
Denunciation, big with conscious might,
And earnest, manly pleadings for the right.

And so the millions, eager to confess
  The pleasures they from his creations drew,
Hastened to praise, and glorify, and bless
  The quiet man whose face they hardly knew,
Who, in his lonely room, worked for his goal,
With busy brain, and strongly-yearning soul;
And with his good pen, built, and rigged, and manned
The noble vessels which his genius planned.

But one dark day, the news flashed o'er the earth,
  That he, belovèd guest of many lands,
Had gone to where his regal soul had birth,
  Led by the pressure of down-reaching hands.
There have been kings, reposing in the shroud,
Scorned in the laughing heart, though mourned aloud;
Here was a citizen, wept by his peers,
And deluged by a flood of heartfelt tears!

'O Dickens! if in yonder star-girt land,
  Thou canst but wander thro' its streets and vales,
And then before the breathless millions stand,
  And tell thy merry and pathetic tales,
If thou canst yet thy daily toil prolong,
Plead for the right, and battle with the wrong,
The happiness of Heaven will o'er thee spread,
For thou thy path Heaven-given, still wilt tread!

No new laudation to thy name we raise—
  No tribute of new grief with us appears;
Through all thy life we gave thee words of praise—
  Long ere thy death we gave thee our best tears.
But wheresoever still the English tongue
In all the world is spoken, read, and sung,
Shall rise the fervent words oft-heard before—
"God bless thee, glorious Dickens, evermore!"

CITY OF BOSTON.

"We only know she sailed away,
And ne'er was heard of more."

Waves of the ocean, that thunder and roar,
Where is the ship that we sent from our shore?
Tell, as ye dash on the quivering strand,
Where is the crew that comes never to land?
Where are the hearts, that unfearing and gay,
Broke from the clasp of affection away?
Where are the faces, that smiling and bright,
Sailed for the death-darkened regions of night?
Waves of the ocean, that thunder and roar,
Where is the ship that we sent from our shore?

Storms of the ocean, that bellow and sweep,
Where are our friends that went forth on the deep?
Where are the faces ye paled with your sneer?
Where are the hearts ye have palsied with fear?
Where is the maiden, so tender and fair?
Where is the father, of silvery hair?

Where is the glory of womanhood's time?
Where the warm blood of man's vigor and prime?
Storms of the ocean, that bellow and pour,
Where is the ship that we sent from our shore?

Birds of the ocean, that scream through the gale,
What have ye seen of a wind-beaten sail?
What have ye heard, in your moments of glee,
Birds of the bitter and treacherous sea?
Perched ye for rest on the threatening mast,
Beaten and shattered and bent by the blast?
Heard ye no message to carry away,
Home to the hearts that are yearning to-day?
Birds of the ocean, that hover and soar,
Where is the ship that we sent from our shore?

Depths of the ocean, that fathomless lie,
What of the crew that no more cometh nigh?
What of the guests that so silently sleep
Low in thy chambers, relentlessly deep?
Cold is the couch they have haplessly won;
Long is the night they have entered upon;
Still must they sleep, till the trumpet o'erhead
Summons the sea to uncover its dead!
Depths of the ocean, with treasures in store,
Where is the ship that we sent from our shore?

God of the ocean, of mercy and power,
Look we to thee in this heart-crushing hour!

Cold was the bitter and merciless wave,
Warm was thy love and thy goodness, to save;
Dark were the tempests that thundered and flew,
Bright was thy smile, bursting happily through;
Bright to the band who have followed thine eye
Home to the shores of the beautiful sky!
Safe in thy goodness and love evermore,
Leave we the ship that we sent from our shore!

LOST AND RECLAIMED.

INTRODUCTION.

Why toil where hands have labored well and long,
Through tears, and blood, and pain?
Why sweep the strings of cold, reluctant song,
And sweep them all in vain?
Why yearn where better hearts have gone for nought,
Through sad, disastrous years,
And seek to earn what has not yet been bought
By reason, prayer, and tears?

There is a fearful demon on this earth,
Stalking from land to land;
Where'er he go, he carries woe and dearth,
And blood-red is his hand.
A million corses mark his cruel way,
And lepers, vile and stained,
Who follow at his bidding, while they pray
To have the devil chained!

They follow him, with footsteps faint and weak,
Through want, and shame, and guile;
They cling to him, they kiss his bloated cheek,
And curse him all the while.
They shrink in horror from his loathsome den,
They dread its hopeless gloom;
They turn and beg deliverance, and then
Rush headlong to their doom.

The sage has drawn the sword of reason out
Against the crafty foe,
And dealt his foul and loathsome form about,
With many a lusty blow;
The orator has mingled in the fray,
The bard has sung his verse;
But victory lingers long upon the way,
And with us stays the curse!

The man of God has raised his tear-stained face
To the Great Priest on high,
And prayed that this fell blight upon our race
Might harmless pass it by;
Yet, for his faith, but slight reward appears;
The guerdon is not won!
Through weary months, and sorrow-laden years,
The fearful work goes on!

And women—they whose cautious, trusting lives
Grow thick with hopes and fears,

The mothers, and the sisters, and the wives—
    Have lavished their best tears;
But tears, alas! have fallen all in vain,
    Or soon to be effaced,
E'en as the dropping of the blessed rain
    Upon a desert waste!

Is there a country hamlet, that has reared
    Its church-spire humbly up,
Where the arch-fiend has not some time appeared,
    And brought the poisoned cup?
Is there a township where, on every hand,
    The wine-cup holds not slaves?
Is there a church-yard in this "Christian land,"
    That counts not drunkards' graves?

Ay, throned within the loftiest halls of state,
    The monster rules the hour,
And in the revels of the rich and great,
    He knows his fatal power.
And gifted men, whom we have named and sought
    To fill the highest place,
Have turned upon us in their shame, and taught
    Us lessons of disgrace!

Shall we submit? Ask you the widow's groan,
    The orphan's helpless cry!
Ask you of those who best the curse have known,
    And mark their stern reply!

Shall we submit? Ask you the crumbling bones
Of victims, fallen low,
And listen to the anguished, pleading tones,
That join in answering, "No!"

By all the glorious records of our race,
Stamped with Jehovah's seal,
By all the humbling lessons of disgrace,
That damp our pride and zeal,
By honest effort, trampled and unknown,
By the glad victor's crown,
By the great truths that deck the Eternal throne,
The monster SHALL go down!

I.

HOME.

O times and manners! hold your way!
You're growing faster every day!
There's naught we heed, or seem to need,
Except the precious boon of speed!
There's naught we seem to care to know,
Except the faculty to go!
And go we must, and "go it blind,"
Or fold our arms, and stay behind.
On railway trains we lie and sleep,
While dragged o'er valley, plain, and steep;

(And so, pet authors we peruse,
And in a kind of mental "snooze,"
We let them drag us where they choose.)
Ah, ancient Dobbin! poor old horse!
Ill luck to thee were Watts and Morse!
Thy usefulness will soon be past;
Thy time, old horse, will come at last!

But let bold Progress have his will!
And let the world grow faster still!
Though poets dream, let engines scream,
And push ahead, with all their steam!
Awhile I leave this noise and strife,
To sing of country scenes and life;
Awhile I sing of country air,
Scented with flowers, so sweet and fair,
Or flaked with snow, when cold winds blow,
And Winter leaves his Northern lair.
Awhile I sing of country roads,
In all their various states and modes;
Of turnpikes, belting hills and vales;
Of croaking frogs, and barking dogs,
And "thank-ye-ma'ams," of logs and rails;
Of level miles, that husband time;
Of hills that horses hate to climb;
Of bridges, o'er ravine and flood;
Of well-made beds of mire and mud;
Of plains, whereon the wheel fast whirls;
Of sidelong slopes that scare the girls;
Who scream so piteously, withal,

And catch at you, with faces blue,
Lest they, perhaps, should catch a fall,
That you, if you have half a heart,
Your prompt assistance must impart,
And tender them your strong right arm,
To keep them safe from mud and harm;
Of guide-posts, showing you along;
Of folks who pass the time of day;
And when you ask of them the way,
They do their best, and tell you wrong!

And then, the grave-yards on the way,
With lettered head-stones, old and gray,
Telling the old, admitted tale—
We know too well the truth they tell!—
That time is short, and flesh is frail.
Telling when youth's bright day-star set;
When dark old age grew darker yet;
When housewives left the wheel and loom,
When rose-cheeked maidens lost their bloom;
When the tired farmer ceased to reap,
And when the baby went to sleep;
When the old doctor, worn and tried,
Went on his last and slowest ride;
When the quaint deacon silent lay
Where he was wont to sing and pray.
When slow, from some death-chilled abode,
The wagons rattled down the road,
Came to the little church, and there
Halted for sermon, hymn, and prayer,

Then bearers, with uncovered head,
Bore the sound sleeper to his bed.

Up such a rustic, quaint old street,
Past field of barley, corn, and wheat,
Past verdant, silver-washed ravine,
'Neath woodland arches, draped with green,
Or, if in wintry day you go,
Past stubble-land and drifting snow,
Past winter-chilled, denuded trees,
Moaning and shivering in the breeze;
Past different homes of different styles,
Ride up the road a dozen miles,
And, passing various homes and names,
You'll come where lived my Uncle James.

It was a sober farm-house, old,
Yet guarded well 'gainst heat and cold,
And looking, on its little knoll,
So quiet, self-possessed, and droll,
That one could almost see it grin
A kind and amiable "Come in."
The beech and maple grew before
Its ancient, hospitable door;
The jessamine, on summer days,
Shut out the hot and piercing rays
That fain would storm the window-frame,
And set the glasses all aflame;
The morning-glory opened up,
Each day, its dainty, purple cup;

And like the hands that bade it grow,
And like the hearts that beat below,
The tender-rooted, fragile vine
Crept slowly round its stated line,
Climbing, each day, with purpose high,
A little nearer to the sky.

Well stocked with hay, and husks, and grain,
Marking the limits of the lane
Halved by a wagon-beaten track,
The surly barn stood coldly back.
Oh, ancient barn! oh, boyhood days!
How stands that place, in homely grace,
Before my retrospective gaze!
How many a day the clover hay,
In treading, tired my boyish legs!
How many a prize my straining eyes
Have found, in hidden nests of eggs!
How well I recollect those sheep;
Each one a shy and woolly heap!
Those orphaned calves, whose nimble tongues
Proclaimed the soundness of their lungs!
The horses—steady, kind old fools;
The biting, kicking, sinful mules;
Whose ways were such, to foe or friend,
That they were safe at neither end!
The cows—especially old Brindle,
A kind of lop-horned, bovine swindle,
Whom Uncle James, one hapless day,
Was milking, and was heard to say,

While Brindle at a thistle picked,
"Now, kick not, that ye be not kicked.
For wherewithal ye kick"—just then
Old Brindle kicked, and kicked again.
Oh, how the pail against a rail
Went crashing on its milky track!
And, king of shames! how Uncle James
Went tumbling over on his back!

The stupid brutes, untaught by Reason's light,
And holding man in awe,
If let alone, will work life's problem right,
And follow Nature's law;
They seek out no inventions; and their skill
Is naught but honest trust;
And that which tends to poison and to kill,
They shrink from in disgust.

They sip the pure, cool dews of eve and morn,
They crop the growing grass;
They feed upon the fresh, green blades of corn,
But never drain the glass!
Some, taught by Nature, live in constant strife,
And on each other prey;
But seldom do they drain each other's life
By slow degrees away!

But man has sought to drown his cares in mirth,
And ignoble desire;
And he has changed the choicest fruits of earth,
To a consuming fire!

And some have revelled in the unholy feast,
And sunk their rank and mark,
Beneath the veriest reptile, bird, or beast,
Of good old Noah's ark!

If so be Reason hold the dumb brute back
From self-destroying greed,
If lack of reason leave him to the track
That Nature has decreed,
If Reason teaches heaven-created man
The arts to make him worse,
(Dispute the doctrine, ye who will or can!)
Then reason is a curse!

Yes, 'tis a curse, (and so is Heaven's best light,)
When showing cursed goals!
Better the darkness of Egyptian night,
Than wrecked and ruined souls!
And he who bears, with sadness or with glee,
Intoxication's fruit,
Were ten times better off, if he could be
A decent, sober brute!

But I must stop this calling names,
And hurry on to Uncle James;
(Called "Uncle Jimmy" by those wights
Who set all names to wrongs or rights,
And follow the irreverent plan,
To nick-name every one they can;)
But there he lived; a fine old man

As e'er the race of Temperance ran;
A well-preserved old man; to whom
Some sixty Junes had shown their bloom,
And sixty winters had appeared,
And frosted o'er his hair and beard.
His high, full brow was creased by care,
And bronzed by Summer heat and air:
His well-set eyes, of deepest hue,
Were clear, and bright, and shrewd, and true;
His beard, with patriarchal grace,
Decked a fair portion of his face;
And his great hands, ne'er known to shirk,
Were hardened o'er with manly work.
Though grief is deep, and years are long,
His gait was upright, straight and strong;
His active mind was balanced, still,
And iron-bound his massive will.
He laid his views of right and sense,
Precisely as he laid a fence:
Marking with care the proper course,
Then building with his utmost force;
And when 'twas done, howe'er it proved,
The fence (or view) was never moved.
For, mind you, when he drove a stake,
The wind might blow, the earth might quake,
He hung steadfastly to his plan,
And never pulled it up again.
Whenever lightning-rods came round,
The glib tongued, well-taught salesman found
In Uncle James, the keenest pill

Of candor, sophistry, and will,
With well-laid grooves for it to follow,
It e'er had been his lot to swallow.
"Why, man alive," he'd say, "the fact is,
Your tall machines won't work, in practice.
There's heaps of lightnin' high in air;
God manufactur's it up there;
And when it comes, the Lord will fetch it,
And then, of course, we'll have to ketch it.
So do you think to frighten God,
Pointin' at Him your lightnin'-rod?
'Twill scare Him just as much, if I
Point my old whip-stock at the sky."

But oh, I wish, some lucky day,
You could have only heard him pray!
I criticise not oft in prayer,
The word, the attitude, or air;
I hold no feud with church or creed;
I blame not those who shout, or read;
But, oh, I wish, some lucky day,
You could have only heard him pray!
His speech was ancient, thick, and slow;
Tinged with the phrase of long ago;
His periods were not free from blame,
His grammar was a little lame;
But oh, his honest, earnest face!
His simple, unaffected grace!
His fervent tone, that seemed to say,
"I'll have the blessing, any way!"

And every word, it seemed to rise
Straight through the ceiling to the skies!

Aunt Rachel was as good a dame
As ever bore that Bible name.
Once glossy ringlets decked her head,
Now streaked with many a silver thread;
Once girlish mischief filled the eyes
Now sorrow-softened, mild and wise;
But never was the heart more true,
And ne'er the eyes of deeper hue,
And ne'er the touch of sharper thrill,
And ne'er the voice of sweeter trill,
That once had made such vexing flames
Within the heart of Uncle James,
Than dwelt in her he yet adored,
Who ruled his house and graced his board.
She ruled by gentle word and scheme,
And she and order reigned supreme,
While kindness governed all her ways,
And kindness lengthened out her days.
When sorrow came, and passed her by,
She pitied much, and looked on high,
And prayed for those round whom it crept,
Shedding her tears with those who wept.
And when the dark-robed ghost of death
Cut short her first-born's feeble breath,
And on the sorrow-clouded day
He wooed her first-born girl away,
And when another son—her pride—

Passed pale and trembling from her side,
She kissed for all each coffined one,
And calmly said, "Thy will be done."

When a dead face lies upturned to the sky,
As ours, God help us! will;
When shadows rest upon the soulless eye,
So helpless and so still;
When the numb hands are crossed and laid away,
In unavailing sleep,
Although we know that form is only clay,
We pity, while we weep.

We pity, that the cold and flushless cheek,
With smiles will ne'er be bright;
We pity, that the tongue can never speak
The words of truth and right;
We pity, that the hand no more may clasp
A friend's, in honor true;
We pity, that it never more can grasp
The work it burned to do!

But do we think what future mortal gain
May gather in the grave?
And do we think what throbs of weary pain
The hand of death may save?
Ay, do we think, while gazing on that cold
And marble-colored face,
That the grim monster may e'en now withhold
The red flush of disgrace?

Better, a thousand times, we early fall,
And perish in the strife,
Than lie beneath intoxication's pall,
And live a dying life!
And the lost drunkard, shouting in his glee,
Or trembling in remorse,
Were ten times better off if he might be
An honorable corse!

But two of all Aunt Rachel's five
Had passed their eighteenth year alive.
Both given to her in one day,
Both since allowed with her to stay.
She marked the manhood of her boy,
Her daughter's loveliness, with joy;
And, weeping thoughts she could not tell,
She thanked her God it was so well.

James, Junior, was a manly lad,
With much to praise, and little bad;
With gay smiles, ever bound to win,
And well-earned whiskers on his chin.
Tall, straight and strong he daily grew,
Each year decreasing what he knew,
As 'twill with any smart young man
Who reads himself, as best he can;
And, on his parents' future page,
James was the staff of their old age.

Some faults, peculiar to his years,
In every growing youth appears.

Good conduct has too much of salt,
Unpeppered by a little fault;
And some few faults, of various names,
Peppered the character of James.
He had a weakness, too, for curls.
And casting sheep's-eyes at the girls;
Especially a black-eyed one,
Brim-full of frolic, sense, and fun,
Full often wild, and never tame,
Admired by all, and Kate by name;
Whom, soberly, he used to seek,
Upon an average, twice a week;
And who, as one might well suppose,
Led him at pleasure by the nose.

But, viewing matters all around,
His traits were good as oft are found.
His country home had kept him clear
Of whisky, brandy, gin, and beer;
His heart was good and well-inclined,
And he was cordial, true, and kind.

Fair Ada, with her mother's face,
Grew up in loveliness and grace.
A simple, trusting maid was she,
Of innocent and trustful glee;
Giving, with heart untouched by guile,
The boon of friendship's hand and smile;
But by grave lessons, early taught,
Knowledge that some have dearly bought,

She knew the dangers of her way,
Guarded herself by night and day,
And, gazing sharply, scanned and proved
The circle in whose bounds she moved.

And so that happy household dwelt,
And toiled, and laughed, and sang, and knelt,
Each morn and eve, before the throne
Where all the deeds of men are known.
And, as they dwelt in that fair place,
Prosperity came down apace,
And gentle love around them twined,
And joined them all, in heart and mind.

II.

LOST.

Was there a bright and glorious Summer sky
　　Ever so pure and clear,
But black and ragged clouds were hovering nigh,
　　To make it dull and drear?
Was there an Eden e'er so blithe and gay,
　　And free from troubling Care,
But hurrying change, some dark, unwelcome day,
　　Brought grief and sorrow there?

When, blessed with pleasant days and fortune's smile,
　　Our life untroubled grows,

'Tis best to guard in watchfulness, the while,
Against unlooked-for foes;
And while we thank the Lord for mercies past,
And blessings, day by day,
'Tis best ahead a watchful eye to cast,
And watch, as well as pray.

Blithe, happy households, basking near and far,
In Pleasure's radiant sun,
Were ominously startled by the jar
Of Sumter's signal-gun;
The nation drew, with anger in its eye,
A long, determined breath,
Then quickly laid its household jewels by,
For scenes of blood and death.

God answered Charleston, with the impetuous rush
Of armed and marshaled men,
Sworn by the waving flag they loved, to crush
The serpent to his den!
And beardless youth, and men of riper age,
With glowing heart and mind,
Turned to life's view a fearful, flashing page,
And left the old behind!

The balls that whiz about the soldier's head,
With danger are replete;
But vastly more the glistening nets that spread
About the soldier's feet!
The carnage-devils, hovering o'er the fight,
Are pitiless and fell;

But vastly more the imps that, day and night,
Would lead the soul to hell!

Was there a camp so guarded round from sin,
And so supremely blest,
But that Intemperance some time entered in,
And made himself a guest?
Are there not those who in the grave are laid,
And still might live to-day,
If those of higher rank, whom they obeyed,
Had spurned the cup away?

The war had come; the stirring call
To save our nation from her fall,
Had issued from the lips of him
Whose honest eyes have since grown dim.
And straight from valley, plain, and hill,
From office, workshop, farm, and mill,
Burning to thwart their country's foes,
Avengers of The Flag arose.
And James, whose heart had often burned,
As records of the past he turned,
Wherein the feuds of former days
Were told in glowing word and phrase,
Felt Freedom's love within him move,
And longed that holy love to prove.

He came, one evening dull and brown,
Back from the nearest market town,
And, entering the lampless gloom

That filled the little sitting-room,
He silent found his parents both;
And told them of the binding oath
That he had taken, on that day,
To mingle in the rising fray,
And do his boyish best to save
The nation from an early grave;
And tearfully before them bent,
Asking their blessing and consent.
The weeping mother did not speak,
But kissed his brow, his lips, his cheek,
Gave him a long and warm embrace,
Then hid her flushed and streaming face.

The father bade the boy to stand;
Then placed his hard and trembling hand
Upon the youthful soldier's head,
And then, in trembling accents, said:
"You're young; and it might better do,
If you might wait a year or two;
For years will come, and years will go,
Ere conquered is that Southern foe;
And we by law might keep you here,
Until you entered manhood's year.
But since you've started on the track,
Go on! we will not hold you back!
Now, do your duty, like a man,
Which means, to do the best you can;
When darkest clouds come o'er your sight,
Look cheerfully ahead for light;

When Pleasure shows her handsome form,
Look out for an approaching storm;
But al'ays, al'ays keep in sight
The good North star of truth and right.
Study, whatever else you do,
Your Bible, and your drill-book, too;
And with the bugle's stirring ring,
Mingle the hymns you used to sing;
And may the God of battles shed
His choicest mercies on your head."

The sister entered, without call—
She paused, she gazed, she knew it all;
And, hastening to the soldier's side,
She mingled tears of grief and pride;
Mingled assurance with her fears,
And smiles of courage with her tears;
And while her gentle eyes grew dim,
She playfully exhorted him
To prove a soldier such as she
Would have her only brother be.

They knelt and prayed; and from the West,
As if the earnest prayer were blest,
Threading a sudden cloud-rift, came
The setting sun's deep, crimson flame;
And through the cottage window, shed
A radiant halo round each head.
But when the fervent prayer was done,
Dark clouds swept swiftly o'er the sun,

And like a deep-toned warning word,
A distant thunder-peal was heard.

* * *

The war went on; the news fast came
Of bloody fights, now old in fame,
Wherein fell many a noble one
Whom fame has never dwelt upon.
Wherein fell many a gallant boy,
Some home's well cherished pride and joy,
Whose noble deeds might well be told
In glowing words of pearl and gold.

But why peruse that blotted page?
Why feel again the lofty rage
That stood in each true face confessed,
And burned in every loyal breast?
Why read again those long death-rolls
That tell of brave, departed souls;
That tell of blazing eyes grown dim;
Of bleeding form and shattered limb?
The war, thank God, is o'er; and we
Live yet, the fruits of peace to see.

The war was done; the priceless boon was saved;
And high, o'er land and sea,
Flashing in bright and star-gemmed beauty, waved
The old flag of the free!
The stifling smoke of battle rolled away,
And tears of joy revealed;

The clanging bells sent forth a roundelay,
And loud the great guns pealed!

Forth marching from the lone, deserted camp,
With proud and glorious name,—
Forth creeping from the prison's deathly damp,
The conquering legions came.
Came, with each past heart-rending woe and grief
Changed to bright pleasure, now;
Came, with the unfading, well-earned laurel wreath
Upon each noble brow!

The household band its rays of comfort shared,
And poured its welcome free,
To those who from the bloody fray were spared,
Their homes again to see.
Maternal love spread wide its yearning arms,
His hand the father gave;
While beauty summoned forth its freshened charms,
To welcome home the brave.

* * *

Come, mother, set the kettle on,
And put the ham and eggs to fry;
Something to eat; and make it neat,
To please our Jamie's mouth and eye;
For Jamie is our son, you know;
The rest have perished long ago!
And when Pat brings him home to-night,
His glad, blue eyes will sparkle bright,

His old, sweet smile will play right free,
His old, loved home once more to see.

I say for't! 'twas a cur'us thing,
  That Jamie wasot maimed or killed!
Four were the years with blood and tears,
  With gloomy, hopeless tidings filled!
And many a night, the past four year,
We've lain within our cottage here,
And while the rain-storm came and went,
We've thought of Jamie, in his tent;
And offered many a silent prayer,
That God would keep him in His care.

I say for't! 'twas a cur'us thing,
  That Jamie was not maimed or killed!
Four were the years, with hopes and fears,
  With long and bloody battles, filled!
And many a morn, the past four year,
We've knelt around our fireside, here,
And while we thought of bleeding ones,
Of blazing towns and smoking guns,
We've thought of him, and breathed a prayer
That God would keep him in His care.

Nay, Ada! you just come away!
  Touch not a dish upon that shelf!
Mother, she knows just how it goes!
  Mother shall set it all herself!
There's nothing, to the wanderer's looks,

Equal to food that Mother cooks;
There's nothing to the wanderer's taste,
Like food where Mother's hand is traced;
Though good the sister's heart and will,
The mother's love is better still.

She knows the side to lay his plate,
She knows the place to set his chair;
Many a day, with spirits gay,
He's talked, and laughed, and eaten there;
And though four years have come and gone,
Our hearts for him beat truly on;
And he shall take, as good as new,
His old place at the table, too!

And 'cross the table, as of old,
Your chair, my Ada, girl, shall be;
Mother, your place, and kind old face,
I'll still have opposite to me.
And we will talk of olden days;
Of all our former words and ways;
And we will tell him what has passed,
Since he, dear boy! was with us last;
And how our eyes have fast grown dim,
Whenever we conversed of him.

And he shall tell us of his fights:
His marches, skirmishes, and all;
Many a tale shall make us pale,
And pity them who had to fall;

And many a one of sportive style,
Will go, perchance, to make us smile;
And when his stories all are done,
And when the evening well is gone,
We'll kneel around the hearth once more,
And thank the Lord the war is o'er.

Hark! there's a step! he's coming now!
  Hark, mother!—there's the sound once more!
Now on our feet, with smiles to greet,
  We'll meet him at the opening door!
It is a heavy step and tone;
Too heavy, far, for one alone;
Perhaps the company extends
To some of his old army friends;
And who they be, or whence they came,
Of course, we'll welcome them the same.

What bear ye on your shoulders, men?
  Is it my Jamie, stark and dead?
What did you say? once more, I pray;—
  I did not gather what you said.
What! drunk!—you tell that lie to me!
What! drunk! O, God! it can not be!
It is, it is, as you have said!
Men, lay him on yon waiting bed!

'Tis Jamie! yes, a bearded man,
  Though bearing still some boyhood's trace;
Stained with the way of reckless days,

Flushed with the wine-cup, is his face;
Swelled with the fruits of reckless years;
Robbed of each look that e'er endears;
Robbed of each trait that e'er might make
Us cherish him for his own sake,
Except the heart-distressing one,
That Jamie is our only son!

Oh, mother! take the kettle off,
And set the ham and eggs away!
What was my crime, and when the time,
That I should live to see this day!
For all the sighs I ever drew,
And all the grief I ever knew,
And all the tears I ever shed
Above our children that are dead,
And all the care that creased my brow,
Are naught to what comes o'er me now!

I would to God, that when those three
We lost, were hidden from our view,
Jamie had died, and by their side
Had lain, all pure and stainless, too!
I would this rain might fall above
The grave of him we joyed to love,
Rather than hear its coming traced
Upon this roof he has disgraced!
But, mother, Ada, come this way,
And let us kneel, and humbly pray.

They knelt and prayed; and God looked down
Upon the cottage old and brown,
Looked on that silver-threaded hair,
Looked on that maiden, young and fair;
And when, with tearful eyes, they rose,
He lightened half their weight of woes.
And though they wept for sorrow, still,
They felt submission to His will.

III.

RECLAIMED.

Next morn the sun rose clear and bright,
And bathed the hills in golden light,
Ere, with a sigh, long-drawn and deep,
The drunkard wakened from his sleep.
No bitter or reproaching word
From those who sought his couch he heard;
They gathered round his curtained bed,
They bathed his hot and aching head;
And when he rose, they vied to prove
The great endurance of their love.
They led him to the teeming board
With relished, old-time dainties stored;
Their studied words were light and free,
And full of well dissembled glee;
But, oh! 'tis hard to jest and smile,
And feel the heart-ache all the while!

Hard for a stream to smoothly flow,
With bitter, boiling springs below!

He ate, and drank, and told full well
The stories soldiers love to tell,
And, waxing warmer, did his best,
With serious tale and sportive jest,
To call the sympathetic tear,
Or bring the hearty laugh and cheer.

At last he came, with cunning tact,
Unto the last night's shameful fact;
And told them how, in army life,
With storms and dire exposure rife,
A drop of liquor, just in time,
Was not considered any crime.
How comrades drank from day to day,
To pass their time and cares away;
How from temptation first he shrank,
And shunned the haunts of those who drank;
Till slow, but surely, thread by thread,
The fatal net was round him spread;
And finally he came to do
That which was wrong enough, he knew,
But which, whene'er once done by men,
Is easier far to do again.
Until his liking for the glass
Had come to such a fatal pass,
That it had come, at last, to fill
The place of balm for every ill.

"But now," continued he, "'tis o'er,
I make myself a sot no more;
And nought of that the drunkard sips,
Shall pass again between my lips."

They knelt, and prayed, and God looked down
Upon the cottage old and brown;
And when they rose, their faces four
With high resolve were covered o'er.
But *one resolve* can never shed
From off one's face the drunkard red;
And *one resolve* can never break
A habit years have gone to make!

O, Habit! ruthless despot! rods of iron,
Are broken every day;
But closer, more relentless bonds environ
The subjects of thy sway!
O, Habit! ruthless despot! bands of steel
Are shattered by a blow;
But closer grasp mankind may never feel,
Than those thy victims know!

O, Habit! cautious safeguard! careful friend!
Watchman by night and day,
To those who to thy fairer regions wend
Their slow and toilsome way!
Happy is he who marks his pathway true,
For right and virtue's sake!
Happy is he who never habit knew,
He would be glad to break!

Scarcely a month had passed away,
When on an idle, careless day,
Habit and appetite conspired
To reach the goal of shame desired,
By one who kept the bane to sell;
A mean, relentless imp of hell;
A poor, unholy child of sin,
With bloated form and senseless grin;
Who held the tempting wine-cup nigh;
Who lived, that better men might die.
O for a word, a word of hate,
To paint this scheming devil's bait!
O for a word, a word of scorn,
To name this poisoned human thorn!
But it was done by crafty men,
And James, poor boy, was drunk again.

Once vows are broken, we may call
Them almost worse than none at all.
But why the doleful tale rehearse?
Poor James went on from bad to worse;
Went on, in spite of tears and sighs,
And bleeding hearts and streaming eyes;
And, every earnest vow forgot,
Became a low, degraded sot.

And yet, some beauty decked his face,
Or lingered still some manly grace,
Or memory of the past came in,
And blotted out the present sin;

For Kate, the black-eyed girl he loved,
Was still by his disgrace unmoved,
And, half in pity, half in pride,
Consented soon to be his bride.
And when they pictured her the life
That hangs about a drunkard's wife,
She, with a true smile, glad and warm,
Replied, "Poor boy! he must reform!
For me he'll drop the fatal cup;
My work shall be to bring him up."

Ah, Kate, beware that fearful length!
Man's weakness has a kind of strength;
And ere you wear the victor's crown,
Look out he does not pull you down!

They married on one hapless day,
And moved a hundred miles away;
And then commenced her patient toil,
To pull from him the leaden coil,
And charm away the magic spell
That hung round him she loved so well.

She labored, toiled, with patience true;
She labored, toiled, all would not do.
Down, down the ladder, still he went,
Until her patience well was spent;
Down, down the ladder, spite of prayer,
And bitter tears, and black despair;

Until *she* turned the fatal leaf,
And madly drank to drown her grief!

And so, devoid of love and shame,
They fellow-revelers became;
And even on their daily board,
The alcoholic mixture poured.
And 'twixt their spells of reckless glee,
Harsh, angry words ran high and free.

At last, one eve, some taunting word
From out her careless lips he heard;
Some word unpardonably true,
That from a drunken quarrel grew;
Whereat a savage oath he swore,
And dashed her fiercely to the floor.

Sobered, she rose; and while the red
Warm blood came dripping from her head,
She turned from him, in bitter spite,
And glided out into the night;
And as she went her way, she swore
Never again to pass his door.

Months came — not she; blood had been found
Upon the floor and on the ground;
Neighbors talked low, from ear to ear,
And coldly said, "Foul play is here;"
And soon the drunken husband saw
Himself within the grasp of law.

Too proud to pass o'er silence's line,
He said no word, he gave no sign;
And when the jury of his life
Proclaimed him murderer of his wife,
He listened, with no word to say,
And heard the Judge pronounce the day,
The place, the manner, and the time
He should be punished for the crime,
And, as the old Judge gravely said,
Hanged by the neck till he was dead.

The morning of the fatal day
Rose heavy-clouded, dull, and gray;
The prisoner's parents, worn and pale,
Were praying with him in his jail;
Ada, her last sad parting o'er,
Had hurried home the day before,
Feeling, she said, she could not stay
So near the horrors of that day.
She sat within her little room,
In bitterest tears and deepest gloom,
When open swung the cottage-gate,
And lo, the pale, sad face of Kate!

"Oh, Ada, can it be to-day,
At noon, so many miles away,
The pitied sight of curious eyes,
My husband for my murder dies?
Far in my recent mountain home,
Where the world's tidings seldom come,

And where, all bent and full of days,
My friend, a gypsy woman, stays,
I, yester-eve, with curious eye,
Watched a boy's kite rise free and high.
'Twas severed from its line; and while
I pondered that full many a mile
The wind had borne its printed sheet,
It fell and fluttered at my feet.
And on the sheet that decked the frame,
I read my poor, dear husband's name;
You know what else — need I say more?
My horse stands foaming at the door;
Another horse must do his half,
And bear me to the telegraph;
Another horse must run, to-day,
To yonder town, ten miles away!"

Away she dashed, through mud and rain;
O'er steep, rough hill, and muddy plain;
But when the ten long miles were past,
And she had reached the goal at last,
She found she was not there too soon;
It only lacked an hour of noon.

The operator stroked his chin,
And answered, with a boyish grin,
"I'm sorry, very sorry, madam;
Your news are good — I wish they had 'em;
If they could go, of course I'd let 'em;
No doubt your husband 'd like to get 'em;

And, laying by all sorts of jesting,
No doubt he'd find 'em interesting;
But as your father-in-law, I take it,
Old Uncle Jimmy, used to make it,
'When lightnin' comes, the Lord will fetch it:
And then, of course, we have to catch it;'
It came in here for keeps, this morning,
Without a half a second's warning;
My battery was torn to flitters —
Likewise, a little flask of bitters;
I found myself, as soon as able,
Snugly laid up beneath the table.
The wires stopped working, quite disgusted;
In short, the whole concern is bu'sted.
But here's an engine, on the track,
Has been somewhere, and just got back;
And this good-looking fellow, here,
A friend of mine, the engineer,
(One of your good, kind-hearted mules,)
Will take you, spite of rain and rules;
Though every cloud were an Inspector,
And every mile-post a Director.
But, Lord! why talk of common things?
At noon, to-day, your husband swings.
'Tis fifty minutes of the time,
And fifty miles! you'll have to climb!"

Now on, iron steed!
  On, on to the goal!
What is the worth of your extra speed,

To the worth of a human soul!
The ground it thunders underneath,
The clouds they thunder above;
On, to the borders of yonder town,
For the sake of the God of love!

My husband must walk out,
To the jailor's nod and beck;
They'll place him upon the gallows high,
With a rope around his neck.
And he will hang and choke,
With deliverance rushing nigh!
On! If ye come not there by noon,
An innocent man must die!

They led the fettered prisoner out,
'Mid pity's tears, and anger's shout;
They led the prisoner out to die,
And placed him on the gallows high.

On! on! on!
The engine shakes and reels;
The rails they quake, they shiver and shake,
Beneath the whirling wheels!
Shake, ye bands of iron!
Roll, ye drivers, roll!
What is the worth of the whole of you,
To the worth of a human soul!

The hangman tied the knot with care,
The good old chaplain breathed a prayer;

The undertaker lingered nigh,
The coffin, rough and black, stood by.

On! on! on!
  With the whistle's screech and scream;
Pile in the coal! pile in the coal!
  And press the hissing steam!
On with the hissing steam!
  In with the senseless coal!
What is the worth of a hundred tons,
  To the worth of a human soul!

Houses and towns fly past, —
  Fly, like a quick-spent breath!
They are naught to us! we are running a race
  With the grim old monster, Death!
On, on with the steam!
  In, in with the coal!
What is OUR flight, in the name of God,
  To the flight of a human soul!

The Sheriff, in a formal way,
Said, "Prisoner, have you aught to say?"
He spoke: his words were clear and plain,
Though mingled with the falling rain;
He spoke: his voice was calm and true,
Though thunder-heads were speaking, too.
"By the great God that dwells on high,
I innocent of murder die;
Guilty of almost all beside,

Cursing my doting parents' pride,
Their every fond wish I have crossed;
I strayed, I wandered, I am lost!
Young men, but listen, while I sum
The secret of my ruin — Rum!
Sheriff, your duty; do not stay!
People, I've nothing more to say."

The good old chaplain breathed a prayer,
Then clambered slowly down the stair.
The Sheriff drew, with manly sighs,
The black cap o'er his prisoner's eyes,
Then turned unto the fatal drop:—
Sheriff, for God's great mercy, stop!

Sheriff, for God's sake, see
  Yon rising column of steam!
Sheriff, for God's sake, hear
  Yon whistle's frenzied scream!
Sheriff, for God's sake, hold!
  What is a moment or two,
To the great, black, eternal gulf
  That meets this prisoner's view?

The spring is touched; the prop is fled;
The prisoner's body falls like lead!

Here we come, at last!
  Come, to sorest need!
Our fifty miles are done and passed,

Thanks to our iron steed!
Fire, and iron, and steam,
Running a race with fate!
Running a race with black-winged Death!
O, Heaven! are we too late?

The rope had broken, as he fell,
And left him there, alive and well;
His face with strangulation dark,
And round his neck an ugly mark,
But living, still, with strength and breath,
As yet untouched by hand of death.
His weeping wife, with streaming face,
Rushed, panting, to his strong embrace;
And the great crowd, on every side,
Like giant babies laughed and cried.

Then, amid silence, clear and high
Arose the prisoner's heartfelt cry:
"O, sacred, generous God above!
To-day, thy grand, forgiving love
Has kept for me my feeble breath,
Has saved my shrinking soul from death!
And now, O God! by all that's dear,
By my loved parents, weeping here,
By her whom thou hast willed to save
Me from a vile, dishonored grave,
By all the scenes of this dread day,
By her, my sister, far away,
By this dread scaffold, dull and drear,

And by the rope that bound me here;
By the black cap across my face,
The blinding badge of my disgrace,
I swear, and send my true oath up,
Never again to drain the cup!
And to thee, God of all, I pray
For strength to battle, day by day;
For heart to strive, and power to win,
Against this fiend of woe and sin."

The rain-clouds burst asunder; and the light
Came streaming gladly down,
As if the smile of God, all beaming bright,
Had chased away His frown!
The wondering multitude stood still as death,
And spoke no wondering word,
And when at last they drew a long, glad breath,
No thunder-peal was heard!

An angel wrote that oath in Heaven's own book,
In gold without alloy;
And Heaven's bright battlements in triumph shook,
With angel shouts of joy.
O'er streets of gold, and verdant, rill-worn plain,
The shining legions flamed,
And sung, in chorus loud, the glad refrain,
"Reclaimed, thank God! reclaimed!"

ASLEEP.

Asleep! asleep! we are all asleep,
From the men who toil to the babes that creep;
From the fiends who lurk where serpents hiss,
To the child that rests with a mother's kiss;
From the youth who courts love's dreamy spell,
To the death-doomed wretch in the prison cell;
From the millionaire on his restless bed,
To the beggar who begs for his daily bread.
Winds may sweep,
And cares may creep,
But wake us not — we are all asleep.

Asleep! asleep! we are all asleep,
And who shall tell of the dreams that creep —
The varied visions of joy and pain,
That toil or dart through the waiting brain?
From the restless lad who yearns to roam,
To the wanderer, dreaming of friends and home;
From the boy who longs for older ways,

To the man, who sighs for his childhood days;
From the maiden who waits for the wedding bell,
To the outcast, shrinking from death and hell!
Passions may leap,
And dreams may creep,
But wake us not — we are all asleep.

Asleep! asleep! we are all asleep;
And who shall tell of the spirits that keep
Their guarding about our silent beds,
Their vigils above unconscious heads?
Of fathers who pity their suffering ones,
Of mothers who weep for their erring sons?
Or who shall tell what mortals lie
Some ghastly phantom hovering nigh,
Some grieved, or ruined, or murdered one,
That curses the form it gazes on?
Ghosts may creep,
And phantoms sweep,
But wake us not — we are all asleep.

Asleep! asleep! not all asleep;
There are those who watch and those who weep;
There are those who long for the tardy dawn,
There are those who pale as the night wears on;
There are those who revel, with giddy brain,
And those who are mourning on beds of pain;
There are those who watch by the sufferer's side,
There are those who wait and creep and hide;
There are those who touch the tuneful lyre,

And those who are fighting the fiend of fire!
Robbers may creep,
And flames may leap —
Though rest be precious, not all may sleep.

Asleep! asleep! we all must sleep,
In a long last slumber, heavy and deep,
'Neath clods of clay and moving forms,
'Neath suns of Summer and moaning storms;
In vaults of marble and nameless graves,
'Neath verdant meadows and ocean waves;
Joining the millions still and dumb,
And waiting the millions yet to come.
Friends may weep,
And troubles may sweep —
They will wake us not from our breathless sleep!

DEAD.

Dead — is she dead?
Has her last mortal word been said?
Has her last precious breath been drawn —
Her soul to join the angels gone?
They tell me, pitying, it is so;
I can not doubt their looks of woe;
And yet, I can not make it seem
That she is dead! 'tis as a dream;
The hard, dull vision of a night,
Ready at morn to take its flight,
Yet mingled with a dreadful fear
That that glad morn may ne'er be here.
  She lies within the narrow case
  That holds her in its close embrace;
Her head with blooming garlands dressed,
Her white hands folded on her breast;
While her pale cheek in color vies
With the long lashes of her eyes.
  But oh, that smile upon her face!
That smile which I have loved so long —

Worshipped, and thought it nothing wrong —
  That smile of beauty, and of grace —
It lingers still! — it stays for me!
  Enters my heart with silent tread,
  And almost lifts its weight of lead;
But O, my God! it cannot be,
  It MUST not be — that she is dead!

And yet they say
That Death has crossed her flowery way.
And they have robed her for the grave,
  With all affection's pompous art,
And mean that sable plumes shall wave,
  And sad friends tearfully bewail
The loss of her who lies in state
Within that polished box of fate,
  Whose every glistening silver nail
  Pricks me unto my very heart!
  And once, when I stood silent here,
  Gazing on all I held most dear,
They paused in their funereal din,
And seemed to think it 'most a sin,
  That I should gaze without a tear!

Tears! tears, indeed!
Would I might shed them; I have need!
Why, I have tears enough shut up
Within my sorrow's aching cup,
  To flood that corse in bitter brine!
For all the tears that e'er were mine,

By all my petty sorrows bred,
Gathered for years but never shed,
Are waiting now to mourn this dead!
They surge and dash against my brain,
They beat, and wear, and give me pain,
  My crippled senses almost drown;
And yet, I fear they must remain,
  For the flood-gates are frozen down!

Dead, surely? — I
Have heard of those who seemed to die,
But in some deadly stupor lay,
And in the grave were laid away.
And how, at last, too late, they woke,
When the dread spell that bound them broke;
Woke, but unto a living death!
  Woke, but to live, and die again!
  And I have heard how they have lain,
  And gnawed their fingers in their pain,
And struggled fearfully for breath;
Then, courting death, have turned them o'er,
And welcomed that they feared before.
Oh, what if she, my loved, my own,
  Should waken in her clayey bed,
With all these friends and mourners flown,
The damp, chill clods upon her thrown—
  The coffin-lid above her head!
Oh, in that horrid moment, she
Would cry, and moan, and call for me!
Oh, blessed thought! would cry for me!

Oh, cursed thought! where should I be?
O God, I can not stand and see
  My angel buried with the dead!

Heavy the long, dark years shall roll
Across my poor, rebellious soul.
Each spring that smiles around me bright,
Will mock me with its merry light;
And when the flowers of Summer start,
They'll mind me of my desert heart,
Where every flower has ceased to bloom —
Where every hope has found a tomb!
When loud the Autumn breezes swell,
They'll sing to me a funeral knell;
And Winter's coldly pinching vise
Will lock my withered heart in ice!
A wretched coward Grief has made,
If I but dared, I too would die,
And with my shattered hopes would lie,
  My last great debt to Nature paid,
Rest for my body she would give;
  But — all my fears and fancies weighed —
I dare not die, I dare not live!

And now, adieu,
The only love that e'er I knew —
  The only love I e'er shall know!
My only one, I press once — thrice —
My burning lips to thine of ice,
  Then turn away in bitter woe;

And now my parting pangs are o'er,
  And I have gazed upon her last,
Close down the coffin lid once more,
  And nail it there, secure and fast.
Then o'er her throw the solemn pall,
  And let me bow my aching head,
Gaze on the holder of my all,
  And make it seem that she is dead.

TO LAKE HURON.

Huron, I stand upon thy shore,
And see thy foaming billows tossed;
I hear thy long-continued roar,
I gaze, I wonder, and am lost!
Lost, in thy waves, that upward leap;
Lost, in thy great, unfathomed deep,
Where human foot hath never trod;
Huron, thou tellest me of God!

Whether the tempest o'er thee lower,
Or sunbeams on thy breast rejoice,
Thou art a token of His power,
Thou art an echo of His voice!
He holds thee in His mighty hand,
He guides thee at His stern command,
Tunes thee to measures soft and light,
And sweeps thy strings with giant might.

The clear blue sky is o'er thee thrown,
Smiling as only Heaven can smile,
And thou below dost sadly moan,
Lashing thy sanded shores the while,
And mourning sadly for the dead

That rest within thy rocky bed;
And as thy waters foam and surge,
Thou sing'st for them a solemn dirge.

For many a vessel, driven afar,
  Has felt the fury of thy wave;
And many a bold and gallant tar
  Has found in thee a gloomy grave.
A thousand hopes too bright to last,
A thousand pictures of the past,
Covered with Sorrow's sable palls,
Lie deep within thy silent halls.

And we, who gaze on thee to-day,
  And walk thy pebbled edge along,
Whiling a social hour away,
  With harmless mirth and cheerful song,
When shall we gather here once more,
To view the wonders of thy shore?
I hear thy voice, old inland sea,
Saying "It nevermore may be!"

And now, old lake, a long farewell!
  Nor Anger's frown, nor Pity's tear,
Nor all the powers of earth and hell,
  Can check thee in thy grand career.
When the Archangel's notes sublime
Proclaim the funeral-rites of Time,
When the last year of earth is o'er,
THEN shalt thou yield, but not before!

APPLE-BLOSSOMS.

Underneath an apple-tree,
  Sat a maiden and her lover;
And the thoughts within her, he
  Yearned, in silence, to discover.
Round them danced the sunbeams bright,
  Green the grass-lawn stretched before them;
While the apple-blossoms white
  Hung in rich profusion o'er them.

Naught within her eyes he read,
  That would tell her mind unto him;
Though their light, he after said,
  Quivered swiftly through and through him;
Till at last his heart burst free
  From the prayer with which 'twas laden,
And he said, "When wilt thou be
  Mine forevermore, fair maiden?"

"When," said she, "the breeze of May
  With white flakes our heads shall cover,

I will be thy brideling gay—
  Thou shalt be my husband-lover."
"How," said he, in sorrow bowed,
  "Can I hope such hopeful weather?
Breeze of May and Winter's cloud
  Do not often fly together."

Quickly as the words he said,
  From the West a wind came sighing,
And on each uncovered head
  Sent the apple-blossoms flying;
"'Flakes of white'! thour't mine," said he,
  "Sooner than thy wish or knowing!"
"Nay, I heard the breeze," quoth she,
  "When in yonder forest blowing."

APPLES GROWING.

Underneath an apple-tree,
  Sat a dame of comely seeming,
With her work upon her knee,
  And her great eyes idly dreaming.
O'er the harvest-acres bright,
  Came her husband's din of reaping;
Near to her, an infant wight
  Through the tangled grass was creeping.

On the branches long and high,
  And the great green apples growing,
Rested she her wandering eye,
  With a retrospective knowing.
"This," she said, "the shelter is,
  Where, when gay and raven-headed,
I consented to be his,
  And our willing hearts were wedded.

"Laughing words and peals of mirth,
  Long are changed to grave endeavor;

Sorrow's winds have swept to earth
  Many a blossomed hope forever.
Thunder-heads have hovered o'er —
  Storms my path have chilled and shaded;
Of the bloom my gay youth bore,
  Some has fruited — more has faded."

Quickly, and amid her sighs,
  Through the grass her baby wrestled,
Smiled on her its father's eyes,
  And unto her bosom nestled.
And with sudden, joyous glee,
  Half the wife's and half the mother's,
"Still the best is left," said she:
  "I have learned to live for others."

THE FADING FLOWER.

There is a chillness in the air —
  A coldness in the smile of day;
And e'en the sunbeam's crimson glare
  Seems shaded with a tinge of gray.

Weary of journeys to and fro,
  The sun low creeps adown the sky;
And on the shivering earth below,
  The long, cold shadows grimly lie.

But there will fall a deeper shade,
  More chilling than the Autumn's breath:
There is a flower that yet must fade,
  And yield its sweetness up to death.

She sits upon the window-seat,
  Musing in mournful silence there,
While on her brow the sunbeams meet,
  And dally with her golden hair.

She gazes on the sea of light
  That overflows the western skies,
Till her great soul seems plumed for flight
  From out the window of her eyes.

Hopes unfulfilled have vexed her breast,
  Sad smiles have checked the rising sigh;
Until her weary heart confessed,
  Reluctantly, that she must die.

And she has thought of all the ties —
  The golden ties — that bind her here;
Of all that she has learned to prize,
  Of all that she has counted dear;

The joys of body, heart, and mind,
  The pleasures that she loves so well;
The grasp of friendship, warm and kind,
  And love's delicious, hallowed spell.

And she has wept, that she must lie
  Beneath the snow-wreaths, drifted deep,
With no fond mother standing nigh,
  To watch her in her silent sleep.

And she has prayed, if it might be
  Within the reach of human skill,
And not averse to Heaven, that she
  Might live a little longer still.

But earthly hope is gone ; and now
  Comes in its place a brighter beam,
Leaving upon her snowy brow
  The impress of a Heavenly dream :

That she, when her frail body yields,
  And fades away to mortal eyes,
Shall burst through Heaven's eternal fields,
  And bloom again — in Paradise.

AUTUMN DAYS.

Yellow, mellow, ripened days,
  Sheltered in a golden coating;
O'er the dreamy, listless haze,
  White and dainty cloudlets floating;
Winking at the blushing trees,
  And the sombre, furrowed fallow;
Smiling at the airy ease
  Of the southward-flying swallow.
Sweet and smiling are thy ways,
Beauteous, golden, Autumn days!

Shivering, quivering, tearful days,
  Fretfully and sadly weeping;
Dreading still, with anxious gaze,
  Icy fetters round thee creeping;
O'er the cheerless, withered plain,
  Woefully and hoarsely calling;
Pelting hail and drenching rain
  On thy scanty vestments falling.
Sad and mournful are thy ways,
Grieving, wailing, Autumn days!

'TIS SNOWING.

FIRST VOICE.

Hurrah! 'tis snowing!
On street and house roof gently cast,
The falling flakes come thick and fast;
They wheel and curve from giddy height,
And speck the chilly air with white!
Come on, come on, ye light-robed storm!
My fire within is blithe and warm,
And brightly glowing!
My robes are thick, my sledge is gay,
My champing steeds impatient neigh,
My many silver bells are clear,
With music for my waiting ear;
And she within — my queenly bride —
Shall sit right gaily at my side;
Hurrah! 'tis snowing!

SECOND VOICE.

Good God! 'tis snowing!
From out the dull and leaden clouds,
The surly storm impatient crowds;

It beats against my fragile door,
It creeps across my cheerless floor;
And through my pantry, void of fare,
And o'er my hearth, so cold and bare,
The wind is blowing;
And she who rests her weary head
Upon our hard and scanty bed,
Prays hopelessly but hopeful still,
For bright Spring sun and whippoorwill;
The damp of death is on her brow;
The frost is at her feet; and now
O God! 'tis snowing!

FIRST VOICE.

Hurrah! 'tis snowing!
Snow on! ye cannot stop our ride,
As o'er the white-paved road we glide;
Past forest trees, thick-draped with snow,
Past white-thatched houses, quaint and low;
Past stately barn and fattened herd,
Past well-filled sleigh and kindly word,
Right gaily going!
Snow on! for when our ride is o'er,
And once again we reach our door,
Our well-filled larder shall provide,
Our cellar door shall open wide;
And while without 'tis cold and drear,
Within, our board shall smile with cheer,
Although 'tis snowing!

SECOND VOICE.

Good God! 'tis snowing!
Rough men now bear, with hurried tread,
My pauper wife unto her bed;
And while, all crushed, but unresigned,
I cringe and follow close behind;
And while my scalding, bitter tears,
The first that stain my manhood's years,
Are freely flowing,
Her waiting grave is open wide,
And into it the snow-flakes glide;
A mattress for her couch they wreathe;
And snow above, and snow beneath,
Must be the bed of her who prayed
The sun might shine where she was laid —
And still 'tis snowing!

THE LITTLE SLEEPER.

There is mourning in the cottage as the twilight shadows fall,
For a little rosewood coffin has been brought into the hall,
And a little pallid sleeper,
In a slumber colder, deeper,
Than her days of life could give her, in its narrow borders lies,
With the sweet and changeful luster ever faded from her eyes.

Since the morning of her coming, but a score of suns had set,
And the strangeness of the dawning of her life is with her yet;
And the dainty lips asunder
Are a little pressed with wonder,
And her smiling bears the traces of a shadow of surprise,
But the wondering soul that made it shines no more from out her eyes.

'Twas a soul upon a journey, and was lost upon its
way;
'Twas a flash of light from Heaven on a tiny piece of
clay;
It was timid, and yet bolder,
It was younger, and yet older,
It was weaker and yet stronger, than this little human
guise,
With the strange, unearthly luster ever faded from its
eyes.

They will bury her, the morrow; they will mourn her
as she died;
I will bury her the morrow, and another by her side:
For the raven hair, but started,
Soon, a maiden would have parted,
Full of fitful joy and sorrow, gladly gay and sadly
wise;
With a dash of joyful mischief in her deep and change-
ful eyes.

I will bury her the morrow, and another by her side:
It shall be a wife and mother, full of love, and care,
and pride;
Full of hope and of misgiving;
Of the joys and griefs of living;
Of the pains of others' being, and the tears of others'
cries;
With the love of God encompassed in her smiling,
weeping eyes.

*

I will bury on the morrow, too, a grandame, wrinkled,
old;
One whose pleasures of the present were the joys that
had been told;
I will bury one whose blessing
Was the transport of caressing
Every joy that she had buried — every lost and broken
prize;
With a little gleam of Heaven in her dim and longing
eyes.

I will joy for her to-morrow, as I see her compassed in;
For the lips now pure and holy might be some time
stained with sin;
And the brow, now white and stainless,
And the heart, now light and painless,
Might have throbbed with guilty passion, and with
sin-encumbered sighs,
Might have surged the sea of brightness in the sweet
and changeful eyes.

Let them bury her to-morrow; let them treasure her
away;
Let the soul go back to Heaven, and the body back to
clay;
Let the grief that here is hidden,
Let the happiness forbidden,
Be forevermore forgotten, and be buried as it dies;
And an angel let us see her, with our sad and weep-
ing eyes.

GONE BEFORE.

Pull up the window-lattice, Jane, and raise me in my
bed,
And trim my beard, and brush my hair, and from
this covering free me,
And brace me back against the wall, and raise my
aching head,
And make me trim, for one I love is coming here
to see me;
Or if she do not see me, Jane, 'twill be that her dear
eyes
Are shut as ne'er they shut before, in all of their
reposing;
For never yet my lowest word has failed of kind
replies,
And ever still my lightest touch has burst her
eyelids' closing;
So let her come to me.

They say she's coming in her sleep — a sleep they cannot break ; —
Ay, let them call, and let them weep, in dull and droning fashion !
Her ear may hear their doleful tones an age and never wake ;
But let me pour into its depth, my words of burning passion !
Ay, let my hot and yearning lips, that long have yearned in vain,
But press her pure and sacred cheek, and wander in her tresses ;
And let my tears no more be lost, but on her forehead rain,
And she will rise and pity me, and soothe me with caresses ;
So let her come to me.

Oh, silver-crested days agone, that wove us in one heart !
Oh, golden future years, that urged our hands to clasp in striving!
There is not that in earth or sky can hold us two apart,
And I of her, and she of me, not long may know depriving!
So bring her here, where I have long in absence pining lain,
While on my fevered weakness crashed the castles of our building ;

And once together, all the woe and weary throbs of pain
That strove to cloud our happiness, shall be its present gilding;
So let her come to me.

* * * * *

They brought her me — they brought her me — they bore her to my bed,
And first I marked her coffin's form, and saw its jewels glisten;
I talked to her, I wept to her, but she was cold and dead —
I prayed to her, and then I knew she was not here to listen.
For Death had wooed and won my love, and carried her away —
How could she know my trusting heart, and then so sadly grieve me!—
Her hand was his, her cheek was his, her lips of ashen gray —
Her heart was never yet for him, however she might leave me;
Her heart was e'er for me.

O waves that well had sunk my life, sweep back to me again!
I will not fight your coming, now, or flee from your pursuing!
But bear me, beat me, dash me to the land of Death, and then

I'll find the love Death stole from me, and scorn him with my wooing!
Oh, I will light his gloomy orbs with jealous, mad surprise,
Oh, I will crush his pride, e'en with the lack of my endeavor;
The while I boldly bear away, from underneath his eyes,
The soul that God had made for me — to lose no more forever;
Ay, she will go with me!

Pull down the window-lattice, Jane, and turn me in my bed,
And not until the set of sun be anxious for my waking;
And ere that hour a robe of light above me shall be spread,
And darkness here shall show me there the morn that now is breaking.
And in one grave let us be laid — my truant love and me —
And side by side shall rest the hearts that once were one in beating;
And soon together and for aye our wedded souls shall be,
And never cloud shall dim again the brightness of our meeting,
Where now she waits for me!

COVER THEM OVER.

FOR DECORATION DAY.

Cover them over with beautiful flowers,
Deck them with garlands, those brothers of ours;
Lying so silent, by night and by day,
Sleeping the years of their manhood away:
Years they had marked for the joys of the brave —
Years they must waste in the moldering grave.
All the bright laurels they waited to bloom
Fell to the earth when they went to the tomb.
Give them the meed they have won in the past —
Give them the honors their future forecast;
Give them the chaplets they won in the strife —
Give them the laurels they lost with their life.
Cover them over, O cover them over,
Parent and husband and brother and lover!
Crown in your hearts those dead heroes of ours,
And cover them over with beautiful flowers!

Cover the faces that motionless lie,
Shut from the blue of the glorious sky;
Faces once decked with the smiles of the gay,

Faces now marked by the frown of decay.
Eyes that looked friendship and love to your own,
Lips that the thoughts of affection made known;
Brows you have soothed in the hour of distress,
Cheeks you have brightened by tender caress.
Oh how they gleamed at the nation's first cry!
Oh how they streamed when they bade you good-by!
Oh how they glowed in the battle's fierce flame!
Oh how they paled when the death-angel came!
Cover them over, O cover them over,
Parent and husband and brother and lover!
Kiss in your hearts those dead heroes of ours,
And cover them over with beautiful flowers!

Cover the hands, that are lying untried,
Crossed on the bosom, and low by the side;
Hands to you, mother, in infancy thrown,
Hands by you, father, clasped close in your own;
Hands where you, sister, when tried and dismayed,
Hung for protection and counsel and aid;
Hands that you, brother, in loyalty knew,
Hands that you, wife, wrung in bitter adieu.
Bravely the musket and saber they bore;
Words of devotion they wrote in their gore;
Grandly they grasped for a garland of light,
Catching the mantle of death-darkened night.
Cover them over, O cover them over,
Parent and husband and brother and lover!
Clasp in your hearts those dead heroes of ours,
And cover them over with beautiful flowers!

Cover the feet, that all weary and torn,
Hither by comrades were tenderly borne;
Feet that have trodden, in flowery ways,
Close by your own, in the old happy days;
Feet that have pressed, in Life's opening morn,
Roses of pleasure, and Death's poisoned thorn.
Swiftly they rushed to the help of the right,
Firmly they stood, in the shock of the fight.
Ne'er shall the enemy's hurrying tramp
Summon them forth from their death-guarded camp;
Ne'er, till the bugle of Gabriel sound,
Will they come out from their couch in the ground.
Cover them over, O cover them over,
Parent and husband and brother and lover!
Rough were the paths of those heroes of ours —
Now cover them over with beautiful flowers!

Cover the hearts that have beaten so high,
Beaten with hopes that were born but to die;
Hearts that have burned in the heat of the fray,
Hearts that have yearned for the homes far away;
Hearts that beat high in the charge's loud tramp,
Hearts that low fell, in the prison's foul damp.
Once they were swelling with courage and will,
Now they are lying all pulseless and still.
Once they were glowing with friendship and love,
Now their great souls have gone soaring above.
Bravely their blood to the nation they gave,
Then in her bosom they found them a grave.
Cover them over, O cover them over,

Parent and husband and brother and lover!
Press to your hearts those dead heroes of ours,
And cover them over with beautiful flowers!

One there is, sleeping in yonder low tomb,
Worthy the brightest of flow'rets that bloom.
Weakness of womanhood's life was her part —
Tenderly strong was her generous heart;
Bravely she stood by the sufferer's side,
Checking the pain and the life-ebbing tide;
Fighting the coming of terrible Death,
Easing the dying man's fluttering breath;
Then, when the strife that had nerved her was o'er,
Calmly she went to where wars are no more.
Voices have blessed her now silent and dumb,
Voices will bless her in long years to come.
Cover her over, O cover her over,
Blessings, like angels, around her shall hover!
Cherish the name of that sister of ours,
And cover her over with beautiful flowers!

Cover the thousands who sleep far away,
Sleep where their friends cannot find them to-day;
They who in mountain and hill-side and dell,
Rest where they wearied, and lie where they fell.
Softly the grass-blade creeps round their repose;
Sweetly above them the wild flow'ret blows;
Zephyrs of freedom fly gently o'erhead,
Whispering names for the patriot dead.
So in our minds we will name them once more,

So in our hearts we will cover them o'er;
Roses and lilies and violets blue,
Bloom in our souls for the brave and the true.
Cover them over, O cover them over,
Parent and husband and brother and lover!
Think of those far-away heroes of ours,
And cover them over with beautiful flowers!

When the long years have rolled slowly away,
E'en to the dawn of earth's funeral day,
When, at the Archangel's trumpet and tread,
Rise up the faces and forms of the dead;
When the great world its last judgment awaits,
When the blue sky shall swing open its gates,
And our long columns march silently through,
Past the Great Captain, for final review,
Then, for the blood that has flowed for the right,
Crowns shall be given, untarnished and bright;
Then the glad ear of each war-martyred son
Proudly shall hear the good judgment, "Well done."
Blessings for garlands shall cover them over,
Parent and husband and brother and lover;
God will reward those dead heroes of ours,
And cover them over with beautiful flowers!

TO SPAIN.

(1868–9.)

O, bright and balmy Spain!
Bright with the sun that decks thy clear blue skies—
Bright with the fire of maidens' wildering eyes;
Bright with the sheen that o'er thy record shines,
And gilds with fame thy mountains, clad with vines!
Bright with the deeds that paled thy ancient foe,
And bade Numantia's smoldering embers glow
In triumph o'er her slain!
Rival of Greece in peaceful ways and arts;
Rival of Rome in brave and warlike hearts;
The home of valor, history long hath told,
That flashed as flashed thy ancient mines of gold,
O, bright and balmy Spain!

O, dark and frowning Spain!
Dark with the ignorance and sin-born ills
That gloom and glower upon thy many hills;
Dark with the crime that taints each passing breeze,

From strong Gibraltar to the Pyrenees;
Red with the blood that meets the dagger's thrust;
Bent with the fruits of recklessness and lust,
And loathsome with their stain;
Trod by the feet of sycophants and slaves;
Festered and blotched by ignominious graves;
While hang above thy wayward, thorny path,
The thunder-heads of GOD's avenging wrath,
O, dark and frowning Spain!

O, grand and glorious Spain!
Grand with the tales thy children love to tell,
Of Ferdinand and peerless Isabel;
Grand as the center of the mighty powers
That humbled proud Grenada's glittering towers;
Land whence Columbus trained his eagle gaze,
And sailed to find a place for Freedom's blaze,
Across the rippling main!
A blaze of light that grows and brightens still,
Like to a watch-fire built upon a hill;
A thing of joy, that patriots love to see;
That shines abroad, and might illumine thee,
O, grand and glorious Spain!

O, crushed and bleeding Spain!
Crushed by the battles of contending foes,
Raining upon thy head their mutual blows;
Crushed by the foreign soldier's reckless tread,
Crushed by the bodies of thy hapless dead;

Crushed by the pall that hid thee from the light;
Crushed by the Inquisition's damning blight,
And priests of lust and gain!
Gnawed by the worms that foul Corruption breeds;
Consumed and wasted by their strifes and greeds;
Upon thy brow humiliation's brand,
Traced by a sceptered harlot's withered hand,
O, crushed and bleeding Spain!

Rouse to thy rights, O Spain!
Ay, thou hast roused, with anger in thy tone,
And hurled thy loathsome ruler from thy throne;
Ay, thou hast roused, with self-reliant trust,
And trod thy haughty nobles in the dust!
Resolve, that ne'er again, whate'er befalls,
Shall hateful Bourbon stand within thy halls,
Or Bourbon's hated train!
Show to the world, whoe'er thy ruler be,
He needs must stand the choice of thine and thee;
Show to the world that every nation's throne,
Whose e'er it be, must be that nation's own!
Show that, O quickened Spain!

Repent, O wicked Spain!
Pray to the GOD thou hast so long ignored,
Not to the virgin whom thou hast adored;
Let natural religion be thy guide,
And not the Pope on whom thou hast relied;
Let Art and Science chase away thy ills,

And perch themselves upon thy many hills,
Improving heart and brain;
Then with a firm but mild and bloodless stroke,
Throw from thy neck the temporary yoke;
And Virtue, Honor, Truth, and Right increased,
Stand forth the grand Republic of the East,
Redeemed, triumphant Spain!

FORWARD.

The beast that counts a heart can feel it beat,
  The man who counts a soul can feel it yearn;
The while it guides his willing, eager feet
  Where triumph calls, and Victory's altars burn.
  The while it prompts his head and hands to earn
That which will place him at the front; the when
  Humanity his merits shall discern,
And give to him a place of honor; then
Acknowledging a man among his fellow-men!

The Fates decreed us at the birth of Time,
  The Fates decree, and hold the fiat still,
That they who cannot or who will not climb,
  Be trampled down by them who can and will.
  Philanthropists may take the doctrine ill,
And nobly lift their suffering fellows high;
  And he who strives to clamber up the hill,
Though weak, has help, for God helps them who try;
But he who will not strive, had best lie down and die!

For hammer, axe, and spade will vex his ears,
  And spindles whirl about his idle head;
The steamer's shriek will rouse his feeble fears,
  The lightning-train will shake him in his bed!
  The nets of cliques and clans will round him spread;
And time — a chariot to the man who strives —
  Will be a funeral car, and he its dead,
Till he unto his charnel-home arrives.
Millions of men have lived good corses all their lives!

A rainbow arches on the clouded sky,
  But ne'er for long its colors flash and play;
A comet shines upon the gazing eye,
  But still is speeding on its endless way.
  Sun, moon and stars — not one of them may stay;
For not an orb — howe'er it seem to stand —
  But marches grandly on by night and day,
Nor cares nor dares to halt, without command
Of Him, the mighty Chief, by whom its route was planned.

A tiny floweret blossoms under foot,
  And turns its dainty petals to the sky;
Draws life from earth and air through leaf and root,
  While yet Destruction broods and lingers nigh;
  But naught that seems inaction we descry,
Though Summer wanes, and Autumn winds are cold;
  When effort fails, the plant is fain to die;
Its energies and days at once are told,
And soon it hangs its head, and crumbles to the mold.

There is not that in earth or air or space,
  There is not that in heart or mind or soul,
Save in one holy and mysterious place,
  But hurries forward to some future goal,
  Or cowers back to an inglorious whole;
Wherefrom it sprung — whereto it turns to die;
  And He who keeps all motion in control,
Whom change and dissolution come not nigh,
The same forevermore — is the great God on high.

Man loves to clamber on the steeps of fame,
  Then rest awhile his wearied limbs; and yet
Each day some fellow-man must learn his name,
  To stand for one who may that name forget;
  Each day some new requirement must be met;
Each changing year his altitude must grow,
  Or, twined about with Comfort's gaudy net,
His indolence may plot his overthrow,
And he may plunge into the deep, dead gulf below.

Yet many a knight who mingles in the broil,
  Falls, ere his sun has reached the highest place;
Death strikes the strongest reaper in his toil,
  And stops the swiftest runner of the race.
  But time is short, and death is no disgrace,
And rather, to the faithful man, a friend;
  And leaves a glory on the marble face
Of him who holds out faithful to the end —
Whose ways are brave and true, so far as they extend.

Then forward, men and women! — let the bell
  Of progress echo through each wakened mind!
Let the grand chorus through our numbers swell —
  Who will not hasten, shall be left behind!
  Who conquers, shall a crown of glory find;
Who falls, if faithful, shall but fall to rise
  Free from the tear-drenched clay that clogs mankind,
To where new triumphs greet his eager eyes;
FORWARD has ever been the watchword of the skies!

WE WAIT.

We all are waiting, and have ever been.
  Upon the steady rock of changeless fate
We sit, and see the foaming waves come in,
And long some treasure of the sea to greet,
Some golden waif, to glitter at our feet;
  We murmur that our ships are over-late,
  And still we wait.

We trace the fragrant path of childhood's days,
  We press our way to manhood's iron gate;
And glorious pictures meet our yearning gaze,
And castles rise, with lofty, gilded dome,
And lure us from the homely halls of home;
  But, nearer viewed, they grow less bright and great,
  And still we wait.

We seize the joyous bloom of manhood's prime,
  We proudly stand within the halls of state;
And gazing higher, steadily we climb,
And pander to the lust of place and power,
And glory in the triumph of an hour;
  We see ahead another sparkling bait,
  And still we wait.

Or, haplessly, we tread life's path awry,
  And gaze from out the prison's guarded grate;
And fiercely glare we at the boundless sky,
And o'er the fields where Freedom joyous roves;
And, pining, view the valleys, hills, and groves;
  And the sick heart beats high with useless hate,
  And still we wait.

Or if upon the field of war we stand,
  And sword with sword for mastery we mate,
Grim Death, and radiant Glory, hand in hand,
Approaching us with silent step we see;
And one of them, we vow, for us must be;
  Bravely we strive to win renown's estate,
  And still we wait.

And when we grope within the gloom of age,
  When our few steps grow feeble and sedate,
We cast our eyes back o'er a blotted page;
We peer among the pictures of the past,
We gaze upon the future, overcast;
  Our musings all with hopes and fears we freight;
  And still we wait.

THE THREE BROTHERS.

Yes, 'twas a terrible, terrible fight,
  With its tumult, rage, and slaughter;
Yes, 'twas a horrible, horrible sight,
  For the blood flowed there like water.
'Twas a victory bought at a fearful price,
  A triumph dimmed in the getting;
And many an eye saw the bright sun rise,
  That saw not the sun at setting.

There were three brothers in that fight —
  The same flag floating o'er them —
While the booming cannon, left and right,
  Crushed all that stood before them.
Fire, and smoke, and hurtling lead
  Hovered in clouds about them;
But together they fought, 'mid the living and dead
  Who ne'er had cause to doubt them.

They saw the enemy onward pour,
  Their death-tubes poised and gleaming,
They heard the belching cannon's roar,
  And the rifle bullet's screaming;

But still they fought with a hearty cheer
  For the friends who lived to love them,
And their every thought was bright and clear
  As the sky that smiled above them.

The eldest, a youth with an eye of fire,
  And a spirit that ne'er was broken,
Was conning the words of his veteran sire,
  The last that to him he had spoken:
"God bless you, my son, as forth you go!
  'Tis well the nation has won you!
But if ever you fall with back to the foe,
  My curses for e'er be on you!"

The second, a youth with a dreamy, brown eye,
  And a form erect but slender,
Thought of a maiden, coy and shy,
  But kind, and loving, and tender.
"My love, I bid thee go," said she:
  "May Fame with her laurels wreathe thee!
Fight for God, and country, and — me,
  And carry this poor heart with thee!"

The youngest, a blue-eyed, fair-haired boy,
  Fought bravely as any other,
But his face lit up with a beautiful joy,
  As he thought of his sainted mother;
How she had soothed his weary woe,
  Ere death had come to sever;
And he thought, "Perhaps, ere the sun is low,
  I shall be with her forever."

Rattled and thundered the brazen guns,
  And pealed the war-cry louder;
Forward rushed the undaunted ones,
  Through dust, and blood, and powder;
Slowly the foe were forced to yield,
  Onward came the others;
But a thousand dead lay on that field,
  And three of them were brothers.

There they lay — by their comrades sought —
  With their good blood all around them.
Side by side they had bravely fought,
  And side by side they found them.
'Mid the wrecks of the battle-storm
  They vainly strove to weather,
Torn and mangled each bloody form,
  They all lay there together.

But I have heard, that upon each face
  Was a smile of manly beauty,
As to say, "I perished in my place,
  And I strove to do my duty."
And I have thought, that in God's good time,
  When a few more years were fleeting,
Far above, in His courts sublime,
  There would be a happy meeting.

THE ARMISTICE.

FEBRUARY, 1871.

Hushed is the sound of the rifle's crash, and the cannon's murderous booming;
Sheathed for a time is the bloody sword, and the flashing bayonet;
Dark on the homes of the ravaged land the war-cloud yet is glooming;
Over the hills of sore defeat, the sun of France is set.
Now on bloody battle-fields of glory and disgrace,
Gaze the nations long and hard into each other's face:
One, with triumph in her eye, sings victory's swelling note,
While her iron hand is tight upon the other's throat.
Under the weight of fell Despair, the conquered one is kneeling,
Gazing upon the conqueror, with anger and surprise;
Yet with a look, half-hidden still, of humble, mute appealing,
Blent with the stern and haughty glance that kindles in her eyes.

*

Close by her cheerless, fireless hearth, a widowed
dame is cowing;
Dead is her son, and dead his sire, and broken is
her heart.
Gloomily o'er her desolate home the cloud of war is
bowing,
While the lightning-bolts of grief from its recesses
dart.
"O my God!" she moans and prays: "let now the
carnage cease!
Kings may quarrel, princes fight, but give the peasant
peace!
Though our legions fall in dust, or march with
triumph's tread,
Will it shut the bleeding wound, or raise the cold and
dead?
Emperor, Regent, President — what boots it which
reign o'er us,
While by our sweat, and tears, and blood, we fill their
glory's cup?
Say! can they raise our fallen sons, to stand again
before us?
Bid our daughters, crushed and shamed, in triumph
to look up?"

Under the temple of his rest, Napoleon's form is lying;
Over its proud and lofty dome the great shot hissed
and fell.
'Neath the shade of the lofty roof, his countrymen are
dying,

Starved by the band that compassed them, and struck
by Prussian shell.
Now the nation crushed and riven at Saalfield's hap-
less fray,
Flings the bolts of bitter hate she forged since that sad
day;
Now she wears the rose that grew on sorrow's quicken-
ing thorn;
Now she pays with usury good the Frenchman's
ancient scorn.
For never an old-time Gaul has stepped into this
strife's arena,
And never chief has France to mass her legions for a
blow;
And never the clash of steel can rouse the conquering
chief of Jena,
And never the Prussians' tread can wake their ancient,
dreaded foe.

So, O France, from the German ground that once by
thee was harrowed,
All the seeds of hate thou sowedst, to thorns of death
have sprung.
So shall thy greedy boundaries by German hands be
narrowed;
This is the fruit thou plantedst when the century was
young.
So, O Prussia, mark thy way, and mind thy rival's
doom:
Plant the seeds of gratitude, while victory is in bloom.

Nations crushed by sword and fire, revenge will some time gain;
Nations crushed by generous deeds, will ever thus remain.
So, if the years to come to thee, shall favor thine ambition,
Or should Defeat thy steps entrap, with shrewd disastrous hand,
Deeds of kindness planted now will meet a blest fruition,
Golden crownèd by the thanks and prayers of France, thy sister-land.

THE RAILROAD HOLOCAUST.

NEW HAMBURG, FEBRUARY, 1871.

Over the length of the beaten track,
Into the darkness, deep and black,
Heavy and fast
Like a mountain blast,
With scream of whistle and clang of gong,
The great train rattled and thundered along.

Travelers, cushioned and sheltered, sat,
Passing the time with doze and chat;
Thinking of naught
With danger fraught,
Whiling the hours with whim and song,
As the great train rattled and thundered along.

Covered and still, the sleepers lay,
Lost to the dangers of the way:
Wandering back,
Adown life's track,
A thousand dreamy scenes among;
And the great train rattled and thundered along.

Heavily breathed the man of care;
Lightly slept the maiden fair;
    And the mother pressed
    Unto her breast
Her beautiful babes, with yearning strong;
And the great train rattled and thundered along.

Shading his eyes with his brawny hand,
Danger ahead the driver scanned;
    And he turned the steam;
    For the red light's gleam
Flashed warning to him there was something wrong;
But the great train rattled and thundered along.

"Down the brakes!" was the driver's shout;
"Down the brakes!" rang the whistle out;
    But the speed was high,
    And the danger nigh,
And Death was waiting with altar and pyre;
And the train dashed into a river of fire.

Into the night the red flames gleamed;
High they crackled and leaped and streamed;
    And the great train loomed
    Like a monster doomed
In the midst of the flames and their vengeful ire —
In the glowing tide of a river of fire.

Roused the sleeper within his bed;
A crash, a plunge, and a gleam of red,

And the sweltering heat
Of his winding sheet
Clung round his form with an agony dire,
And he moaned and died in a river of fire.

And they who were spared from the fearful death,
Thanked God for life, with quickened breath,
And groaned that too late
From their terrible fate
To rescue their comrades was their desire;
They sank in a river of death and fire.

Pity for those who woke and died,
And sank in the river's merciless tide;
And blessings enfold
The driver bold,
Who, daring for honor, and not for hire,
Went down with his train in the river of fire.

DEAD AND ALIVE.

The biting, wintry storm swept swiftly round,
And wrapped the cottage in its chilly folds,
Thatching it thicker every icy hour.
The tiny snow-flakes fluttered in the wind,
Careered, and dashed, and fell, and rose again,
As fain, each one, to live its longest time,
Ere sinking back to an inglorious whole,
Lost, nevermore a snow-flake.

Every thing
Bore, on that day, the signet of King Death.
The clouds were palls, and every drift a shroud.
The apple-trees were singing funeral hymns;
And high the leafless burghers of the wood
Rose, 'mid the storm, like skeletons upright.
Death reigned without the cottage, and within
E'en held his somber court.

The house was still,
E'en to the burly clock; whose lumbering weight
So oft had climbed, responsive to HER touch.
The tell-tale hands had stopped, the hour she died,

And, mutely eloquent, e'en yet proclaimed
The fatal time that saw her life go out.
The time that tuned the hopeless, dreary wail
Of many sad and motherless young hearts,
Chilled as with ice by three remorseless words:
" Your mother's dead."

Ah! many friends we love
Must part the clouds of earth, and seek the sky,
Ere we can fly to find where they are gone.
The earth may beat on many a coffin lid
Fit time to strains of sorrow in our hearts,
For those upon whose lifeless forms it falls.
Life's turnpike teems with sorrow's flinty stones,
And takes its toll in sobs and bitter tears,
For those who faint and fall upon the way.
And yet, a hundred griefs may come and go;
Each in its turn may bend us to the earth;
And then, while yet we mourn the latest ill,
Some crushing sorrow may outweigh them all.

It is a sad, a mournful thing, to see
A cherished sister lying in her shroud;
To feel no more the confidence and love
That hung upon her pure and hallowed lips;
To know that Death, a suitor come unbid,
Has wooed her from your strong, encircling arm;
To feel a hundred flowers of memory nipped
By the same frost that rests upon her brow;
To think of all the past — the darling past —

The blessed past — as all forever gone,
Without a future to renew its charms;
Ah, yes! a sister's loss is hard to bear!
And yet, it is not all.

A brother's grave
Is fenced and girt with desolation round.
There is no sound so mournful as the hush
That broods and lingers o'er a death-stilled heart;
And there is power, and mighty power, to move,
With the inaction of a strong right arm.
For memory lingers, in her double guise,
Rewarding and avenging all the past;
Pouring a blessed balm for some kind word,
And giving thrusts for each unworthy deed.
Ah, yes! a brother's loss is hard to bear!
And yet, it is not all.

A father's voice
May hush its words of counsel and reproof,
Its blessings, and its hopeful words of cheer,
And sink in Silence's dark, unfathomed sea.
A father's coffin holds a treasure lost;
A father's love is something strong and true,
A father's loss is heavy to be borne!
And yet it is not all.

But oh, the pang,
The cruel pang, the hard, heart-sickening pang,
That turns each sweet of life to bitterest gall,

Each zephyr to a tempest, and each breeze
To organ-tones of woe ; the hopeless pang
That pits rebellious life against itself,
When the strong cord, the golden, love-charged cord
That binds a faithful mother's heart to ours,
Severs, and falls in ruin at our feet,
And mocks us, with its brightness, from the dust!
There is no loss, except the loss of Heaven,
Like that which fills a loving mother's shroud.
There is no love, except the love of God,
Like that which burns within a mother's heart.

It is a fire that never will go out,
Though base ingratitude be on it poured;
Though wickedness may wrap and clasp it round.
E'en he who checks the answer to its prayers,
Still sees, along his crooked, thorny path,
The mild refulgence of its constant light.
And though he tread the vilest steeps of sin,
And climb, perchance, with wayward, bloody stride,
E'en to the hangman's rope, a mother's lips
Will kiss him in his coffin of disgrace,
And dote on him for what he might have been.

And there she lay — the mother of that flock —
Unheeding all the childish tears of grief,
That else had wasted not a single note,
Without her loving and consoling kiss.
The hearth was cold — the kitchen fire gone out —
And the bold storm beat madly at the door,

Like some importunate mourner, that would fain
Admittance gain, to sorrow with the rest.

While yet the stricken band were closing round,
And weeping sorrow that they could not tell,
The door swung swiftly on its creaking hinge;
And, heeding not the sudden, wondering look
Of the sad father, as he raised his eyes
And sighed for sorrow of the hopeless past,
Entered a young and fragile female form,
With locks dishevelled, and with garments thin,
And face as pale as she had been the dead.
Upon her brow were drawn long lines of care,
And marks that told of waywardness and vice.
Scarce greeting them whose wondering looks she met,
She hastened to the sleeper; and with tears
Of penitence, that well might pay the debt
That sin and disobedience had run up,
She clasped the stiffened form unto her breast,
And madly kissed the mute, unanswering lips,
And thus she spoke:

"O mother, mother, lost!
Thou're here, and yet thou'rt gone! I still can see
The gentle smile that lingers on thy face,
But cannot hear thy kind, consoling voice!
My lips impure may kiss thy sacred cheek,
Yet feel no kindly pressure back again!
My words of grief and penitence may fall

With pardon humbly asked, upon thine ear;
And yet thou canst not hear them; and no word
Of blest forgiveness canst thou answer back!

"O mother, mother wronged!
Wronged by ingratitude, and all the shame
That one like me could heap upon thy pride!
Wronged by neglect, and bitter, scornful words!
Spurned, when thou followedst me, e'en in my guilt,
Down to the darkest depths of wayward sin,
And begged of me, with tears, to come with thee,
And tread the paths of virtue once again!

"Speak to me but one word; one little word
Of pardon, for the dark and shameful past;
One little, fleeting word; nay, e'en a breath;
Or give to me a sign; a smile; a look;
That I may feel forgiveness for my sin!
I cannot see thee laid into thy grave,
Without one word of pardon or of love!
And if, O God! Thou wilt but let her come,
But just to speak one little word to me,
I swear to Thee, my lips shall sing Thy praise,
My heart shall beat accordance with Thy word,
And truth and virtue shall adorn my life,
Until this weary heart shall cease to beat."

As the frail plantlet, bursting from its seed,
Casts off the earth that rests upon its head,
And springs to blooming beauty, so this prayer,

Cleaving the guilt and shame that o'er it hung,
Bloomed fair and pure before the All-seeing eye.
And it was answered. From her deathly trance,
The mother woke; and, lifting up her head,
Said, "Where am I? a deep, long sleep was mine.
I dreamed that in the fields of Paradise,
A shepherdess, I watched and fed my flock;
Till the Almighty came to me and said,
'Matron, return unto thy flock below;
For they are chilled by the cold, wintry storm;
And one, which long time went from thee astray,
Worn, soiled, but penitent, to-day returns.
She shall be washed in the pure blood of Christ,
And thou shalt take her, chastened, to thine arms."

WE HOPE.

With the sunlight, with the moonlight, with the star-
light sweet and golden,
Come to us a thousand memories that are true, and
kind, and olden;
And we enter in the chambers of our hearts so gladly
lighted,
And with blooming hopes we cover all the joys that
care hath blighted,
And encouraged, and rejoicing, we go forth upon
our way.

With the midnight, with the storm-cloud, with the
darkness fiercely scowling,
With the rattling of the rain-drops, and the tempest's
dismal howling,
Through our weary hearts, in darkness, we go halt-
ing, stumbling, groping,
While Despair is hard upon us, and e'en covers up
our hoping;
And in sadness, and in silence, for a gleam of light
we pray.

Then we yearn and call for comfort; but no comfort
comes unto us,
And we wrap ourselves in sadness, and Despair goes
thrilling thro' us;
And the darkness gathers rounds us, with its horrors,
half-unspoken,
And we pray again for succor: that the fearful spell
be broken,
With the light of something shining, be it only but
a ray.

Then within our hearts a blossom, from the dreary
mould is springing,
Then the birds of Hope make music, with their sweet
and cheerful singing;
Then, upon the great clouds gazing, we discern their
silver lining,
And at last, through veils of blackness, bursts the sun-
beam's glorious shining,
And upon our raptured vision beams the light of
perfect day.

CONTENTS.

www.ingramcontent.com/pod-product-compliance
Lightning Source LLC
LaVergne TN
LVHW021412110826
845150LV00007B/1888

* 9 7 8 1 4 2 5 5 1 0 7 1 8 *